CONTENTS

ABOUT THE AUTHOR   vii

PREFACE   ix

PART I

Establishing the Literacy–Mathematics Connection

CHAPTER 1   3

Building the Connection

CHAPTER 2   18

Using Children's Literature and Other Texts to Support Mathematical Learning

PART II

The Connection in Action: Improving Mathematical Skills While Fostering Literacy Growth

CHAPTER 3   43

Strengthening Writing Skills While Communicating Mathematical Knowledge

CHAPTER 4   67

Creating Powerful Poetry About Mathematical Concepts

CHAPTER 5   94

Enhancing Oral Communication Skills With Mathematical Talk

CHAPTER 6   129

Viewing and Visually Representing Mathematical Information

APPENDIX A   163
IRA/NCTE Standards for the English Language Arts

APPENDIX B   165
NCTM Standards for Mathematics

APPENDIX C   169
An Annotated Bibliography of Recently Published Mathematical Trade Books

APPENDIX D   177
Professional Resources

REFERENCES   181

INDEX   189

Literacy + Math = Creative Connections in the Elementary Classroom

Jennifer L. Altieri

The curricular barrier that has long separated math and literacy instruction is an artificial one.

INTERNATIONAL
Reading Association
800 BARKSDALE ROAD, PO BOX 8139
NEWARK, DE 19714-8139, USA
www.reading.org

The International Reading Association attempts, through its publications, to provide a forum for a wide spectrum of opinions on reading. This policy permits divergent viewpoints without implying the endorsement of the Association.

Executive Editor, Books   Corinne M. Mooney
Developmental Editor   Charlene M. Nichols
Developmental Editor   Tori Mello Bachman
Developmental Editor   Stacey L. Reid
Editorial Production Manager   Shannon T. Fortner
Design and Composition Manager   Anette Schuetz

Project Editors   Stacey L. Reid and Wesley Ford

Cover   Design, Brad Tillinghast; Photograph, © 2009 Jupiterimages Corporation

Library of Congress Cataloging-in-Publication Data

Altieri, Jennifer L.
  Literacy + math = creative connections in the elementary classroom / by Jennifer L. Altieri.
    p. cm.
  Includes bibliographical references and index.
  ISBN 978-0-87207-475-0
  1. Language arts (Elementary) 2. Language arts--Correlation with content subjects. 3.
Mathematics--Study and teaching (Elementary) I. Title. II. Title: Literacy plus math equal creative connections in the elementary classroom.
  LB1576.A61575 2010
  372.6--dc22

                                                                                    2009044473

To Ashley, Audrey, Erin, and Natalie

ABOUT THE AUTHOR

**Jennifer L. Altieri** is an associate professor and coordinator of the Division of Literacy Education in the School of Education at The Citadel in Charleston, South Carolina, USA. She is a coauthor of *Moving Toward an Integrated Curriculum in Early Childhood Education*, which was published by the National Education Association. She has also published articles in *Teaching Children Mathematics, Teaching Exceptional Children, Reading Psychology, Reading Research and Instruction*, and other professional journals.

After completing a BS in Elementary Education at Bowling Green State University, Ohio, she moved to Houston, Texas. There she taught in the Aldine Independent School District and Spring Independent School District. Jennifer has served as a reading consultant for elementary and middle schools in the St. Louis Public School District and University City School District in St. Louis, Missouri, and at Port Royal Elementary in Beaufort, South Carolina. She has conducted workshops at the elementary and middle school levels on a variety of literacy topics and is known for her enthusiasm and sense of humor.

Jennifer earned her MEd from the University of Houston and her PhD from Texas A&M University. Along with serving on *Reading Horizons*'s editorial board and the International Reading Association (IRA) 2010 Standards Committee, she regularly presents at IRA conventions.

She resides in Mt. Pleasant, South Carolina. When she is not working, Jennifer spends her time traveling internationally, beating harmless little yellow balls on the tennis court, and enjoying life in Charleston with her bulldog and pug.

Author Information for Correspondence

Jennifer welcomes your questions and comments. Please feel free to contact her at jennifer.altieri@citadel.edu.

PREFACE

We often reflect on our past experiences in life to better understand our current position. Looking back on my own life, it seems that my interest in writing a book related to mathematics and literacy began approximately 10 years ago when I worked with preservice teachers at Saint Louis University. At that time, I was teaching a variety of literacy education courses to elementary education majors. As part of their literacy education courses, I would encourage cross-curricular integration when preservice teachers taught lessons at a local professional development elementary school. I repeatedly saw lessons in which literacy development connected with content areas, yet math was rarely one of the content areas preservice teachers chose to integrate. Therefore, as I found myself focusing on helping preservice teachers integrate the content areas, I became more interested in the literacy–mathematics connection in the elementary grades.

About this same time, I began working with teachers in the field as a reading consultant, and it was clear that the development of literacy skills often was not tied to the teaching of mathematical concepts. However, I believed that strong literacy teaching could enhance students' learning in mathematics.

As can be seen in the National Council of Teachers of Mathematics's (NCTM; 2000) *Principles and Standards for School Mathematics*, the teaching of math has changed drastically over the years. The focus has shifted to hands-on activities, building a community of learners, and relating math to the world around us. Likewise, the literacy community encourages authentic reading and writing, collaborative learning, and activities that foster real-world connections. Students are expected to read with a clear purpose in mind and use writing as a tool to communicate their knowledge. Teachers often encourage flexible grouping and help students see that literacy is a skill that extends beyond the classroom.

Therefore, I believe that by strengthening the literacy–mathematics connection, the teaching of mathematics will be more enjoyable and more relevant to students. In order to be contributing members of society, we constantly must use both math and literacy skills to meet our needs. As adults, it isn't possible to separate the two skills in day-to-day tasks, and therefore we should not expect that of children. Strengthening the literacy–mathematics connection will not only improve math skills but also provide additional opportunities and experiences to foster literacy growth.

Even though there are many excellent content area textbooks available for educators, most of the ideas and suggestions contained within these books are often applied to social studies or subjects other than mathematics. In fact, it appears that very little has been written in the educational field that is designed to foster the connection between mathematics and literacy. My hope is that this book helps start the dialogue regarding the literacy–mathematics connection. By helping students see the powerful link that can exist between the two areas, we are not only developing literacy skills but also reinforcing their mathematical knowledge.

Although some of the literacy strategies presented within this text may not be new, it is highly likely that educators have not seen these strategies applied specifically to the field of mathematics. Many educators may not have thought about enhancing literacy and mathematical knowledge through oral debates, poetry, and student-created visuals. Along with those activities, there are less familiar games, a graphic organizer designed to assist students with understanding vocabulary found in word problems, and other activities that many teachers can try for the first time.

An Overview of the Book: Fitting the Pieces Together
· ·
Organizing everything in nice, neat, little boxes is impossible with real-life learning. Enhancing literacy knowledge and mathematical understanding requires an overlap of ideas. Learning can't be broken down into isolated little segments. Literacy is messy—in a good way. Language skills are so complex and intertwined that it is impossible to share an activity and then say that it develops only listening or talking skills. Therefore, I share within each chapter how specific activities focus on the aspect of literacy discussed. However, most of the activities mentioned develop many aspects of literacy. The reader will also find at the end of each chapter a section titled "Where Do I Go From Here?" Its purpose is not only to offer closing thoughts for the chapter but also to provide ideas to help readers see the relevance and applicability of the information in their own classroom and professional lives.

When people think about connecting literacy and mathematics, many immediately think about word problems. Although word problems can be difficult for students, the literacy connection is about so much more. The purpose of this book is to help expand this limited view of the literacy–mathematics connection. Therefore, Part I, which includes Chapters 1 and 2, discusses the basics and the foundational knowledge necessary for creating the connection, and Part II, Chapters 3–6, shares with the reader a wide range of practical applications for implementing the information.

In Chapter 1, "Building the Connection," we begin to examine the literacy–mathematics connection. I start by explaining what I mean by the term *literacy*, which is a complex idea to explain. This book is based on a broad view of literacy because I feel it is important that we address all aspects of literacy when working with students to prepare them not only for functioning but also for thriving in the world around them. Although we often choose to separate different aspects of the curriculum, these divisions often are not seen by the eyes of our students. Issues that create barriers between the integration of math and literacy are addressed, and numerous benefits of making the connection are outlined. We also take a look at the principles and standards of the NCTM (2000), the standards for the English language arts (International Reading Association [IRA] & National Council of Teachers of English [NCTE], 1996), and commonalities that exist between the two. By familiarizing oneself with these math and English language arts standards, it is easy to understand how they can provide a strong foundation for the learning that takes place in the classroom. As educators, we can assist our students with making connections between literacy and mathematics and simultaneously provide meaningful learning experiences.

Whereas all of the chapters mention specific texts that might be tied into math and literacy activities, in Chapter 2, "Using Children's Literature and Other Texts to Support Mathematical Learning," a variety of texts that may support the connection are examined. Texts are discussed in the broadest sense of the word. Along with sharing specific criteria for selecting mathematical trade books to use in classrooms, there is a discussion of other texts that might enhance instruction. Ideas for the use of local and imported texts in the classroom are detailed. There are numerous options for materials that can connect literacy and mathematics.

Part II expands on the foundational information in Part I by providing specific activities and instructional strategies for enhancing literacy growth while also increasing mathematical knowledge. Chapter 3, "Strengthening Writing Skills While Communicating Mathematical Knowledge," presents a variety of strategies that encourage students to reflect and write on their mathematical knowledge. Because writing doesn't need to be a solitary event, many of the ideas discussed in this chapter encourage students to write with others. Similar to the ideas shared in Chapter 2, all of the activities and ideas within Chapter 3 not only allow students to connect and communicate mathematical knowledge but also can be used to monitor growth in both literacy and mathematical skills.

As we move on to Chapter 4, "Creating Powerful Poetry About Mathematical Concepts," we find a section dedicated to helping students learn to write a variety of mathematical poetry. When one thinks of writing and mathematics, poetry rarely comes to mind. Yet I believe that poetry is one of the best ways to encourage the connection between literacy and mathematics. Since the idea is new to many teachers, this entire chapter is dedicated to making that connection. The chapter begins with a look at the definition of poetry and our purpose for tying poetry into the mathematics curriculum. Then we take a look at some of the simplest formula poems, which are easy to use with even the youngest of students, and a variety of poetry types are shared. From those poetic forms, we move on to riddles. After that, more challenging types of poetry, such as those with multiple voices and preposition poems, are discussed. Educators can find examples of poetry that can be used with a variety of ages.

In Chapter 5, "Enhancing Oral Communication Skills With Mathematical Talk," we discuss how to foster growth within two aspects of literacy—talking and listening—that are often left to develop on their own. This is especially true with upper elementary students. Since talking and listening are not specifically assessed on most standardized tests, and students are able to talk and listen long before formal schooling starts, we often expect those skills to develop at an acceptable pace without direct instruction. However, the articulation of thought and effective listening are extremely important for making a difference in the world. In this chapter, ideas are shared to foster the development from less formal types of oral communication, such as conversations, to more formal types, including debates and interviews.

Finally, in Chapter 6, "Viewing and Visually Representing Mathematical Information," we learn about two of the newest aspects of literacy that were added to IRA and NCTE's English language arts standards in 1996: viewing and visually representing. When we hear those terms, many of us immediately think of drawing. Although drawing is not uncommon in mathematics, this chapter is about much more. The reader is exposed to various ideas for simultaneously developing viewing skills and mathematical skills. Also discussed are ways that students can show their mathematical understanding through a variety of visual representations.

Although it is impossible to include samples from all elementary grades within each chapter, a range of grades is shown whenever possible. Samples from kindergarten to sixth grade are shared, and many of the ideas discussed can easily be modified and integrated into any elementary classroom. Although actual teacher and student names are replaced with pseudonyms, the spelling and writing of the students is not modified. Student samples found in figures and text are replications of the students' actual writing.

Within the different chapters, various standards are addressed through the activities and examples shared. For additional information on the English language arts standards or the NCTM standards, the reader can look at Appendixes A and B, respectively. In Appendix C, a number of excellent children's mathematical trade books published since 2005 are shared, so educators can enhance students' literacy development and build their mathematical knowledge. If further information is desired to help make the literacy–mathematics connection, Appendix D includes other professional sources that educators might find valuable, along with a number of professional journals and books written for educators.

There are many benefits to having a broad conceptualization of literacy. By developing all aspects of literacy, we can better meet the needs of the students entering our classrooms. Not only will we appeal to diverse learners but we will also connect with students' out-of-school literacy experiences by making the idea of literacy a much more relevant concept.

It is no secret that math and literacy are two areas that are gaining more and more attention in elementary schools. In fact, when I talk to teachers, they often state that most of their instructional time is dedicated to teaching mathematics and reading. However, these same teachers are confronted with increased curricular expectations, rigorous standards, and the pressure to demonstrate that their students are performing well on assessments. As the field of education grows more complex, creating connections among math and literacy is vital for educators who work within the constraints of an already busy schedule. Instructional feasibility is often (and wisely so) one of the most important issues with teachers. By tying reading, writing, oral language communication, and visual literacy to mathematics, we reinforce the math skills that students must develop and also enhance their literacy skills. As is shown throughout this book, standards from both areas can be introduced, developed, and reinforced through engaging lessons.

By sharing practical ideas and activities, it is my hope that beginning and experienced teachers, who may not currently integrate mathematics and literacy, find the support necessary to make the connection. For those educators who are already integrating the two fields, it is hoped that this text provides additional ideas to strengthen the connection already present.

Acknowledgments

I have been fortunate to work with many amazing preservice teachers, practicing teachers, and principals over the years. They have all influenced me and helped me gain new ideas and insights into learning. One such person is Carol Schyllander, whose sixth-grade classroom in the Toledo Public Schools provided me with one of my first experiences in the "real world" of education. She continued to educate me for the next 20 years by sharing her life of teaching through letters and photos. Furthermore, Beth Hedrick, my graduate student and advisee, who completed her master of education degree at the age of 80, continues to show me that learning is truly a lifelong process.

I especially want to thank Kristen Wright, Kelly Lozier, Ashley Pfeffer, Betsy Nichols, Sara Buckley, Charles Manning Blakely, Rhonda Richmond, Amy Treneff, Angie Grimes, Sarah Coyne, Annette Hill, Beven Nichols, Jamie Albritton, Lauren Wilson, Charlotte Wilson, and all of the other teachers who took time out of their busy schedules to work with me and listen to my ideas. Dan Ouzts, Tony Johnson, and Roger Stewart constantly remind me of the power of laughter and the necessity to keep life in perspective. Judy Hagen, Kathy Triggs, and Alice Hambright make my job easier on a daily basis, so I have the time to write.

Of course, no book is possible without the feedback and guidance of others. Therefore, I appreciate all of the assistance I received from Corinne Mooney, Anne Fullerton, Wesley Ford, and Stacey Reid at IRA.

However, the real value of any book lies within the reader. Given the busy world we have today, I want to thank you for taking the time to read this book and think about how the ideas within might pertain to your classroom. I look forward to hearing from you!

PART I

Establishing the Literacy–Mathematics Connection

CHAPTER 1

Building the Connection

Before focusing on particular strategies or activities that integrate mathematics and literacy, it is important to take the time to clarify what is meant by the *literacy–mathematics connection*. In this chapter, I examine literacy and mathematics expectations and the barriers that often stop us from making a connection between the two. By understanding the goals and purposes for each subject area, it is easier to see the potential benefits that exist from connecting the two.

Defining Literacy

Let's first look at the definition of literacy. For anyone in the educational field, it is obvious that the meaning has changed a great deal over the years. Many years ago, a person was considered literate if that person could read and write, and those were the skills that were highly valued when anyone referred to literacy. Therefore, educators focused the majority of their time and energies on developing students' ability to do so.

Talking and listening skills were sometimes encouraged in the youngest grades through activities such as show-and-tell, but otherwise it was expected that those skills could be developed naturally without any type of educational focus. And why wouldn't we assume that? Because children learn to talk and listen at home as toddlers, many believed that these weren't skills that needed to take up limited classroom time. Furthermore, talking and listening had never been a focus of standardized tests, and often the content necessary to be successful on those exams is given priority in the classroom.

In fact, talking and listening skills were not only marginalized in educational settings but also talking was highly discouraged. A great deal of learning occurred in isolation without involvement with peers. Students were not in the classroom to have conversations with their peers—that was best left to lunch, recess, and physical education class. Instead, the common view was that students were in school to learn, and to maximize learning the classroom needed to be full of quiet workers. The goal was quiet classrooms where students were busy working on tasks.

However, times have changed. To begin with, there is now an obvious focus in schools on collaboration and cooperative learning. Along with peers talking among themselves, the idea of facilitating growth in oral language skills is becoming more common. Through research in the field, it is clear that we need to focus our attention on oral language skills, and we need to give talking and listening their share of time in the curriculum. Research shows that all aspects of literacy are related. In fact, children with weaker oral skills (Loban, 1976) often are not as effective with their writing.

As educators, we now realize that to create citizens that can not only function in the present world but also become contributing and successful members of society, we need to help students learn to speak in an articulate manner that is appropriate for the situation, their goals, and the audience. It is also important that students can listen effectively to others, perceive biases or propaganda techniques being used, and comprehend what they are hearing. Therefore, our literacy goal must be to support students in becoming effective communicators within the classroom context and outside the school setting. As the world becomes more complex, that task becomes even more challenging.

Whereas language arts has historically comprised reading, writing, talking, and listening, *Standards for the English Language Arts* (International Reading Association [IRA] & National Council of Teachers of English [NCTE], 1996) expanded beyond those areas to include viewing and visually representing (Tompkins, 2009) as the six areas of literacy. Not only must students be able to read, write, talk, and listen effectively but also they must be able to understand what they view around them. To do this, students need the opportunity to interact with a variety of texts. Although textbooks, children's books, and other print-based media are important and have their place in the classroom, a lot of information can be gained from commercials, the Internet, films, and videos. Students must also apply metacognitive skills with these forms of text and be educated viewers.

Along with comprehending the material that they view, students need to visually represent and communicate information for various audiences to share information in a variety of ways, including through the nonprint media of drama, posters, charts, video productions, and a wide range of other visuals. Visually representing information, as with other forms of communication, requires that students think about the information they want to convey, understand the audience who will view the creation, and determine the most effective way to share the information.

To be effective as literacy educators, we must work hard to assist students with all six aspects of literacy: reading, writing, talking, listening, viewing, and visually representing. No longer can the focus of classrooms be on traditional communicative arts. This broad-based view of literacy is the basis for this text. Preparing students for the world in which they live is not an easy task. However, unless we believe in a broad conceptualization of literacy, it is an impossible task.

Rethinking the Curricular Barriers We Create

Over the years, the value of creating cross-curriculum integration has been well documented in the literature. Educators show that an integrated curriculum is often more motivating for the learner than the traditional way of teaching (Guthrie, Anderson, Alao, & Rinehart, 1999). Not only is the content more interesting but also, when connections are made between content areas, students can more easily remember the information for problem-solving tasks later (Nuthall, 1999). Boaler's (2008) research examines how math is taught at a number of schools, including Railside High School where students are taught in a communicative approach. The students learn to communicate mathematics through a variety of methods, including words and visual representations. Students also work collaboratively within the classroom. The results are amazing. Yet even with these studies, it appears the literacy–mathematics connections often are not made in classrooms. To make the connections, we must examine and understand why they are not currently occurring.

The topic of content area literacy is not new. For years, those involved in the educational community have researched, written, and encouraged the integration of literacy skills into other areas of the curriculum. Although many excellent books have been written (e.g., Alvermann, Phelps, & Gillis, 2006; Conley, 2007; Moore, Moore, Cunningham, & Cunningham, 2006), the majority of strategies and samples shared in those texts are not tied into mathematical content. It seems almost as if there is an invisible barrier separating mathematics and literacy. According to Harvey and Goudvis

(2007), teachers have been asking for more information on incorporating reading strategies through the mathematics connection for many years. Although obtaining the information is vital, even more important is examining how we view the content areas. We must each rethink our compartmentalization of different content areas in order for the information to be of value.

When we look at the content areas in elementary schools, one thing is clear: Even when elementary school teachers team-teach subjects, often science and math are paired together, as are social studies and language arts. This trend continues into the middle school setting. I rarely, if ever, have a practicing teacher in my graduate classes who teaches language arts and mathematics.

For adults, there appears to be a certain degree of uncertainty or uneasiness associated with merging the two fields. However, students do not see the barrier between two subjects until adults separate them by materials, time, and sometimes teachers. In fact, as Moyer (2000) states, "The separation of language and mathematics instruction in the elementary grades is very unnatural for children" (p. 255). According to her, "The world of a child involves patterns, problem solving, communication and connections" (p. 255). As adults, we must rethink our own views on the separation of those two areas to align our views with that of our youngest students. So much more learning can occur and be reinforced when we integrate the curriculum.

When we look at the learning occurring outside the educational context, we see rich learning experiences in which students must incorporate knowledge from a variety of areas. If someone wants to shop, the task requires knowledge of a complex set of skills that can't be broken down into distinct, separate topics. It is necessary to reflect on what we have heard or seen in various media to determine what we might purchase. We are often involved in writing a list, reading product descriptions and sale flyers, comparing prices and determining the cost of items, and computing the total amount owed. In the same manner, a complex set of skills is needed to view a favorite movie, plan a party, and spend a day at the zoo. If a family wants to take a trip, they read road maps and determine directions, analyze distance and time, and calculate expenses. Each of these activities demands a strong foundation in mathematics and literacy.

However, historically we have felt the need to separate the areas within the school setting. Traditionally education has felt the need to break the day and curriculum into distinct parts. Scholars describe a typical day in secondary schools as being broken up into certain periods of time, with teachers isolated within their own classrooms teaching the content for which they are responsible, and the classrooms located within a certain physical space (Moje, 2008). For the most part, this can also describe many elementary and middle schools. The unnatural barrier that separates the two fields of study needs to be removed. Only by removing these barriers will students see the relationship between what they learn in school and what occurs in their homes and communities.

Literacy and the IRA/NCTE Standards

This broad view of literacy has been strongly advocated and supported by two professional organizations, IRA and the NCTE. Together, these two professional organizations developed the standards for the English language arts (IRA & NCTE, 1996), which are presented in Appendix A. More information about the standards also can be found by visiting the websites for each organization: www.reading.org and www.ncte.org.

Although these standards are shown in a list, it is clearly noted that language is complex and cannot be broken down into 12 distinct areas. The standards are overlapping and interweaving and not independent of one another. These interrelated standards focus on fostering the necessary literacy skills for students to become functioning and contributing members of society. The only way to do this is to provide a wide range of literacy experiences. Educators are expected to use their knowledge and creativity to provide those important experiences for their students. The standards are not seen as an end product but rather as part of the process. Through reflection and discussion of the standards, educators can share their visions of the truly literate student who will be ready to partake in and influence an ever-changing world.

Certain assumptions are clear with these standards. Literacy skills emerge and begin developing long before students enter a school setting and will continue to develop outside of the educational setting. Thus, educators must build on the literacy skills that students possess. It is evident that language is truly multimodal (Leland & Harste, 1994). Therefore, in the same manner, standards will weave themselves through the various aspects of literacy discussed, and likewise each chapter in this book focuses on the system of meaning (i.e., reading, writing, talking, listening, viewing, and visually representing) that the activities within each highlight, but no activities can occur isolated from other systems of meaning.

Mathematics and the NCTM Standards

The view of mathematical knowledge and skills has changed a great deal over the years. Along with a stronger emphasis on hands-on activities and higher level thinking, technology is also seen as important to the way that mathematics is taught and learned. Students are expected to be able to communicate their mathematical thinking and reasoning to a wide audience instead of focusing on obtaining a correct answer to a textbook problem. Individual work completed in isolation and lists of repetitive problems are no longer as highly valued. Instead, establishing a classroom community is encouraged during mathematics lessons. The classroom is a source of collaborative work, a variety of printed materials, and authentic experiences that connect to the outside world. These changing expectations are due in large part to the principles and standards of the National Council of Teachers of Mathematics (NCTM; 2000). This organization focuses on mathematics in the same way that the NCTE and IRA focus on the field of literacy.

The principles and standards of the NCTM (2000) provide a strong foundation for mathematical learning and show what students should know and be able to do from prekindergarten through grade 12. Within this document, there are a total of 10 standards, 5 of which are content standards that articulate the mathematical content that students should understand. The other 5 are process standards: Problem Solving, Reasoning and Proof, Communication, Connections, and Representation. These 10 standards further explain the educator's role in helping students meet the mathematical standards. Although these standards are listed in Appendix B, by visiting NCTM's website, www.nctm.org, it is possible to review a more detailed description of them, see specific classroom examples, and gain a better understanding of what these standards mean for each grade range.

Commonalities of the Standards for Mathematics and Literacy

Whereas the content standards refer to broad areas that all students must learn within the field of mathematics (i.e., number and operations, algebra, geometry, measurement, and data analysis and probability), the process standards show educators what students must be able to do. These process standards can easily be connected with literacy. Problem Solving and Reasoning and Proof can be facilitated through the traditional communicative arts. Through reading, writing, talking, and listening, teachers can help students develop those processes. Two of the other process standards, Communication and Connections, provide natural links between literacy and mathematics. The Communication Standard requires that students be able to organize and effectively communicate their mathematical ideas. Students must be able to articulate mathematical information to a variety of audiences and comprehend the information that others share. To be able to carry out this communication, students must have a solid knowledge of the academic vocabulary and the necessary mathematical language.

The Connections Standard requires that students make connections to other aspects of their life and use their mathematical knowledge outside of the mathematics classroom. Therefore, teachers must build out-of-school connections and provide links that show students the relevance of their learning to the world around them.

Finally, the Representation Standard involves the ability to use visual representations to communicate mathematical knowledge with others. Similar to the other process standards, it is not enough to understand mathematical material; decisions must be made regarding the medium used and the audience that will view the information. Students must determine the best way to organize this knowledge and present their ideas. This standard ties closely to the viewing and visually representing aspect of literacy.

Through the guidance provided by the NCTM standards, educators can make informed decisions about the teaching of mathematics in the classroom. All of these standards are tied together through six overarching principles: equity, curriculum, teaching, learning, assessment, and technology. By understanding, reflecting on, and sharing these ideas with colleagues, it is expected that teachers can best prepare students for the lifelong mathematical knowledge they will need.

It is evident that there are many commonalities between both sets of standards, and these commonalities make fostering the connection between literacy and mathematics that much easier and important. It is readily apparent that neither set of professional standards is prescriptive or narrow in focus. Both sets allow for the creativity and professional knowledge that teachers possess. Educators need their background knowledge and experiences to produce creative and worthwhile lessons. There is no "one shoe fits all" philosophy with either set of standards. Education is complex, and luckily there are many outstanding educators who will go the extra distance to ensure that students have motivating and challenging educational lessons. These standards can serve as the basis for the lessons.

The two professional communities that developed the standards share common goals for the students. Both sets of standards are designed to ensure that students develop skills and abilities necessary to participate as productive members of society. The goal for both math and literacy standards is to start with what students know, then build on preexisting knowledge and experiences. By reflecting on what students bring into the classroom and extending classroom learning back into the world, we are fostering a deeper understanding of both content areas.

Incorporating Technology

The standards for English language arts clearly articulate the value of technology. In the overall purpose, the standards state that the definition of *texts* has broadened to include print and nonprint media. Nonprint media represents many different aspects of technology, including videos, the Internet, and even television and radio commercials. Plus, viewing and visually representing are key areas that encourage the integration of technology. Students must be able to understand what they see and be able to represent their knowledge in a variety of formats.

Likewise, technology is one of the principles that guide the NCTM's beliefs about classroom mathematics. The process standards state that prekindergarten through grade 12 students should be able to communicate and connect their mathematical knowledge. This was not easy in the past when few schools had access to technology. However, according to the National Center for Education Statistics (2002), 99% of schools have Internet access. Using technology in the classroom is now becoming a reality. Although technology in the past was often limited to educational games that students could play on a classroom computer to practice skills, this is no longer true. Students are motivated and interested in technology because it is often a part of their everyday lives. In fact, students are much more knowledgeable about technology than many adults because the students grew up with it.

To be considered truly literate today, students must be able to thrive in the technologically advanced world in which they live. They must not only understand the technology that is currently available but also be flexible and educated enough to adapt to the constantly changing technological landscape. To be confident in this integration of technology throughout their daily lives, students need to see the same types of connections made in the classroom. As technology continues to play a larger role in our world, it is imperative that students learn to use technology for a variety of purposes. Instead of just layering technology on top of the already existing classroom curriculum, we must integrate technology within the curriculum (Smolin & Lawless, 2003). Because many students use technology outside of school, technology is often a motivator that connects learning from students' homes and communities to the school.

Emphasizing the Needs of All Learners

The IRA/NCTE standards stress the importance of meeting the needs of all students. As the world continues to change, our classrooms become more culturally and linguistically diverse. With this diversity, we must continually monitor how we are reaching all students by building on the richness that our students bring to the classroom and accepting the challenges their differences present for meeting the standards. Whereas the standards provide the foundation of what we want all students to learn and be able to do, the process by which we achieve the desired results can take a number of paths and turns. This book is written to aid in that process by providing a variety of ideas and strategies to help educators navigate the journey.

Benefits of Building a Connection Between Literacy and Mathematics Instruction

Since we have reviewed the standards for both literacy and mathematics, examined the changing views of the two content areas, and looked at what is hindering the connection between them, let's now look at some of the benefits that can be gained by making the connection. Although the obvious gains are enhanced literacy skills and a stronger understanding of mathematical content, there are less obvious but very important benefits of strengthening the connection. The following sections outline key areas where we will see positive effects from integrating the curriculum.

Enhances Instructional Feasibility

As we all know, there never seems to be enough hours during the school day to teach all of the content areas. Teachers often feel overwhelmed by all of the requirements they must meet during the academic year. Often teachers get stressed and burned out professionally due to these requirements. We feel that we must be able to state which area of the curriculum is being taught and which standards are being met during separate times of the day, which creates an unnecessary burden on educators. However, by creating natural connections between literacy and mathematics, we can develop and reinforce important skills throughout the curriculum. The additional focus spent on each area and the natural connections made within the curriculum will enable teachers to feel that they are better able to give adequate instructional time to literacy and mathematics.

Facilitates Student Collaboration

Although we often read about the value of collaboration and cooperative learning, facilitating small groups requires planning by the teacher. To begin with, teachers must think about what they want to accomplish with a lesson or activity. If the ultimate goal is to have the students repeatedly practice a certain skill, then perhaps having students work together in small groups isn't the best idea for that particular activity. However, if teachers want students to interact while solving a problem and make interpretations, students can benefit from working in small groups (Nystrand, Gamoran, & Heck, 1993).

Although students can work in collaborative groups during any type of academic instruction, collaboration seems to occur naturally when we connect literacy with content areas. As we focus more on what Leland and Harste (1994) refer to as "whole literacy," it is easy to facilitate the completion of activities and projects in a variety of collaborative groups. Some activities may be done individually, but many others are best completed through working with partners or in small groups. Collaboration is important, since rarely as adults do we work solo to complete tasks. We almost always receive feedback, such that even the most basic activities in the real world often involve input, support, and ideas from others.

Prepares Teachers and Students for the Reality of Standardized Testing

Standardized tests continue to receive a lot of attention. Although we don't want to teach to the test or make tests the focus of our teaching, we do want to prepare our students to be successful on the exams. Just as teaching mathematics has changed over the years, the mathematics tests have changed. They are no longer focusing on the memorization of rules and requiring students to simply determine the answer. Students must be able to read and understand the question being asked, reflect on what they already know to determine how best to solve the problem, and communicate this understanding to others. Research shows that we must focus on developing students' academic language due to the realities of standardized testing and accountability (Fitzgerald, 1995). Also, students must effectively use literacy skills for authentic purposes, such as considering goals, understanding the audience, and effectively communicating ideas. Strengthening literacy skills and providing activities in which students have an opportunity to apply those skills in a mathematical context can prepare students for standardized tests.

Provides Authentic Learning Experiences

Educators seek to provide all students with authentic learning situations, but completing worksheets and filling in blanks does not achieve this. As adults, we seldom sit and complete math problems simply for the sake of doing math problems. Likewise, as adults we are not called upon to select the grammatically correct form of a word that best completes a sentence or write definitions for a list of terms. Therefore we must seek activities that integrate all six areas of literacy (as outlined in the "Defining Literacy" section at the beginning of this chapter) and provide opportunities for students to develop their mathematical skills in meaningful ways. These activities should reflect and extend the experiences that students have in their own communities and homes, so the students learn information that will be important to them outside of the educational context and are prepared for the world.

Encourages Community Involvement

Often parents and community members do not feel as if they are part of the school community and may hesitate to get involved with their children's classrooms or even visit the school. However, this involvement is crucial for the creation of a successful classroom community. Perhaps the adults had early schooling experiences that were negative or feel they don't have anything of value to share. The adults may also have limited English proficiency. When parents fail to get involved, they cannot share their concerns and may feel marginalized. Parents are on the outside looking in at the experts (educators) who are teaching the children. However, in a truly integrated curriculum, we want to encourage the connection to the community. Even for parents and guardians who cannot physically come to the school, the community can be connected through the extension activities that students share outside of the classroom. The adults must realize that they are an integral part of the learning community and valued in the classroom.

Many of the mathematical activities that incorporate various aspects of literacy development will be strengthened with family and community members' input. Adults can relate their experiences with using math on a daily basis, assist students in the creation of mathematical trade books, or share print and mathematical visuals that play a role in their daily lives. Teachers may even want to look into using literacy tutors to support their students' work. These tutors may include grandparents and other family members, local college students, faith-based organizations, or even local businesses that have an interest in working with students (Al Otaiba &

Pappamihiel, 2005). When the curriculum is looked at more holistically, and the connection is made across mathematics and literacy, the natural connection to the community comes easily.

Reaches the Culturally and Linguistically Diverse Learners

According to all of the reports, our schools are becoming more culturally and linguistically diverse. The U.S. Census Bureau (2001) shows that in 2000, more than 4 million English learners (ELs) were in our classrooms. This does not necessarily mean that the students in our schools have immigrated from other countries. In fact, 76% of ELs in our schools were actually born in the United States (Capps et al., 2005). However, all of these students will bring with them unique experiences and backgrounds.

At a time when our schools are becoming more diverse, the demands of diversity are creating additional issues for ELs. Research shows that the literacy-based math performance assessments are causing some ELs to be unable to demonstrate their true abilities (Brown, 2005). DiGisi and Fleming (2005) find that EL students need additional support in order to be able to read and respond to questions on open-ended assessments. The results of a longitudinal study completed with Latino families (Lopez, Gallimore, Garnier, & Reese, 2007) suggest that "literacy and numeracy proficiency go hand in hand, and to close the Latino mathematics achievement gap a combined effort of preschool and early elementary literacy and numeracy interventions programs are needed" (p. 456).

Many of the recommendations for ELs fit well with the suggestions provided in this book for integrating literacy and math instruction. Sheltered instruction—a research-based approach for working with ELs—focuses on cooperative learning and fostering of academic language, the use of hands-on activities and visual aids, and building on students' background experiences (Hansen-Thomas, 2008). These are all strategies that can be easily integrated through connecting literacy and mathematics and are encouraged in this text.

Also, according to Hansen-Thomas (2008), it is vital that teachers reinforce concepts that may be more difficult for ELs. Concepts, such as homonyms or multimeaning words (e.g., *scale, yard, volume, pie,* and *product*), and homophones (e.g., *weight/wait* and *sum/some*) can prove more difficult for ELs to understand. However, it is easier to develop academic language and content area vocabulary in an integrated curriculum that focuses on connecting literacy and mathematics skills.

Supports Various Styles of Learning

Many students learn in ways that may not be supported within the academic context. As adults, we often describe ourselves as auditory learners or visual learners. Therefore, instead of expecting all students to learn in a particular way, it is important to teach the way that students learn. By incorporating literacy across mathematics, we allow students to reach their potential by learning and sharing through a variety of means. According to an article by Moran, Kornhaber, and Gardner (2006), there are nine types of intelligence: linguistic, logical-mathematical, musical, visual-spatial, bodily-kinesthetic, naturalistic, interpersonal, intrapersonal, and existential. To best meet the needs of the students present in our classrooms, we need to provide rich experiences in which the students are allowed to interact in a meaningful way with the content (Moran et al., 2006). When educators provide experiences that connect literacy and mathematics, it is easier to foster the multiple intelligences (Drake, 1998).

Although we realize that students have individual strengths and weaknesses, we don't want to limit their options by viewing each of the intelligences as black-and-white. Instead, learning styles should serve as a guide when designing a variety of experiences that fulfill the diversity of needs we find within our classrooms. Once again the flexibility and variety provided through the connection enable students to enhance their literacy skills and understand mathematical concepts.

WHERE DO I GO FROM HERE?

The purpose of this book is to assist teachers, literacy coaches, and reading specialists in making the connection between literacy and math, two of the most valued and tested areas of the curriculum in our schools. Whereas educational reform has been discussed for years, the most recent professional standards for the English language arts and mathematics clearly show the importance the professional organizations are placing on cross-curricular learning. This type of integrated learning is essential for students to effectively communicate their mathematical knowledge and apply it to situations beyond the classroom.

As parents, community members, administrators, and teachers work together to achieve this goal, it will truly help students understand what it means to be literate. It is no longer enough to be able to read and write. We must prepare students who can articulate their views, listen appropriately, understand what they see, and represent their learning through a variety of ways. There is no single approach or best way to accomplish this. However, the following chapters will provide ideas for facilitating this connection. Educators must be creative and flexible as they continue to prepare students for the world in which they live. Through collaboration and hard work, we can move theory into practice.

CHAPTER 2

Using Children's Literature and Other Texts to Support Mathematical Learning

H istorically, basal series have been the primary material for reading instruction since they became popular in the 1840s. Over the years, they drew a lot of criticism for the content (Durkin, 1981), vocabulary (Chall, 1983), and instructions provided for the teacher (Woodward, 1986). As time passed, many teachers became interested in integrating children's literature into the classroom, and the reading basal changed to adapt to the market. In 1993, new literature-based basal series were published. The publishers of these texts not only included already-published stories written by children's authors but also encouraged the incorporation of children's literature into the reading classroom (Hoffman et al., 1994).

A parallel modification of materials and incorporation of literature into the classroom were also evident in mathematics instruction. For many years, elementary teachers used math textbooks as the primary texts, and often the only texts, when developing mathematical understanding. The purpose of the textbooks wasn't to encourage students to discuss, reflect, and talk about what was in the book. Instead—as many of us can remember—students worked to complete numerous pages of practice problems included in the chapters, and often the answers were listed in the back of the books. If there were any type of classroom discussion surrounding the text, it often involved the teacher giving the answers and the students determining if the problems were correct (Tanner & Casados, 1998). I still remember the lack of enthusiasm and interest my own elementary students showed when they were asked to take out their mathematics textbooks, and I was not much more eager than they were for mathematics.

Having looked at recent math textbooks, it is apparent that the publishers have changed the books over time. They are no longer filled with rote problems that students mindlessly sit and complete. Many mathematical textbooks designed for elementary teachers now include lists of suggested children's books that can be tied into mathematical lessons, and these lists also provide ideas for additional materials that might be incorporated into the activities. Since we have seen changes in math and literacy textbooks and materials over the years, we now have an added professional responsibility. With the changes in curricular resources, there are more decisions to be made by the teacher. As educators, we must draw upon our professional knowledge and expertise to make decisions about which materials to use in our lessons. To do this, we must take into consideration the students' needs and our educational goals, then determine the best way to integrate the materials into our lessons.

We are already aware of the importance of developing competent readers and using diverse texts with literacy lessons. Standards 1 and 2 for the English language arts (IRA & NCTE, 1996; see Appendix A) discuss the wide variety of materials that students should be able to comprehend. In addition, Standard 6 states that students should be able to "create, critique, and discuss" texts (p. 3). Through integrating these types of diverse materials into lessons targeting mathematical concepts, we provide our students with additional opportunities to connect mathematics with the world outside the educational setting and see reading as a valuable means to communicate information across the curriculum. Students understand that literacy and math are not separate and discrete parts of the day but instead that learning is interrelated. This literacy–mathematics connection encourages students to read various materials for authentic purposes. By supplementing our hands-on math lessons with diverse texts, including quality children's books, we are enhancing both reading and mathematical skills.

The purpose of this chapter is to help educators locate and select materials that will connect reading and mathematics. Along with children's books, this chapter discusses other forms of print media that can enhance mathematical lessons. This includes what Maloch, Hoffman, and Patterson (2004) refer to as local texts, which are "written texts created or constructed by classroom participants" that are "both a part of and a reflection of those social practices" (p. 147), and imported texts, which are children's literature and a variety of other materials brought into the classroom. Also, there are guidelines that can help teachers determine which texts to select for lessons. For those educators who are already using a variety of materials to develop mathematical concepts, this chapter provides additional ideas for incorporating the materials into lessons and shares some new texts that teachers might want to consider for their students.

Supplementing mathematical lessons with other forms of text beyond the standard textbook helps students see the relevance of mathematics within their daily lives. Often, published textbooks and workbooks are written with the assumption that students have common experiences and language. Students who are not part of the mainstream may have more difficulties with such materials (Moll, 1990). Using other types of materials allows teachers to customize lessons based on students' experiences.

Children's Literature Genres for Developing Mathematical Understandings

Educators and researchers strongly support the use of children's literature in the classroom. High-quality children's literature allows teachers to model fluent reading, broaden readers' experiences to new situations and people who may be different from them, and build a love of reading (Kiefer, Hepler, & Hickman, 2006; Norton & Norton, 2002; Smith & Bowers, 1989). Through this type of literature, we can create tasks that encourage students to explore mathematical concepts (Braddon, Hall, & Taylor, 1993).

There are currently large numbers of trade books being published that teachers might choose to integrate into the math curriculum. The volume of books being produced may be partly due to mathematics being seen as a profitable area in which to publish. If teacher editions of math textbooks are providing lists of children's books to use with lessons, then obviously there is a lucrative market for the children's books. It is amazing, but probably not surprising, that many publishers of textbooks and other materials are also now creating series of trade books. In fact, many large publishing companies are mass-producing books for almost every mathematical concept. For example, Children's Press publishes both Scholastic News Nonfiction Readers and Rookie Read-About Math books. DK Publishing has an entire series, Math Made Easy, and SandCastle's Let's Measure series has numerous books that are each written on a different type of measurement. Weekly Reader, a popular name with educators, markets a number of mathematical trade books, and Marshall Cavendish Benchmark has a series called Math All Around.

As we know, quantity is not synonymous with quality. The number of books we use in our classroom is not nearly as important as their quality. Although time constraints placed on teachers can be daunting, taking the time to review and select texts that engage students, broaden their realm of experiences, and make them think is time well spent.

It is no secret that textbooks can appear overwhelming to many students, many of whom have a math phobia similar to writer's block. Students worry that they will not be successful when presented with an intimidating textbook. By selecting quality children's literature, a medium many students love, the teacher can bridge the gap and enable students to realize that mathematical concepts are attainable. Although a wide variety of children's books are available, many teachers are not using them (Moyer, 2000). The purpose of this chapter is to ensure that teachers feel comfortable with selecting and integrating a wide range of materials to make the literacy–mathematics connection.

Although there are numerous books that can be incorporated across content areas, the children's literature focused on in this chapter were written with the intent of developing mathematical understanding. This type of literature includes concept, counting, poetry, story, and informational books.

Concept Books

Concept books are designed primarily to teach or reinforce concepts. Often they do not have a plot and have very few words. The books might focus on a concept as basic as a shape or a number or as complex as decimal points and percentages, such as in *Piece = Part = Portion: Fractions = Decimals = Percents* (Gifford, 2003). Each page of this concept book shows a photograph of a part of something. The reader might see the part as eggs in a carton or one toe peeking out of a pair of socks. Then the author states the amount shown in the photograph in fractions, decimals, and percentages.

Other books that reinforce and teach mathematical concepts may have more words, but the intent of the author is to develop mathematical knowledge. *Round Is a Mooncake: A Book of Shapes* (Thong, 2000) is an excellent picture book that teaches children about a variety of shapes and where they may be seen. It is told in rhyme and includes basic information about the Chinese culture. A page in the back of the book shares even more knowledge about the Chinese elements in the book.

Counting Books

Although counting books are primarily used in early elementary classrooms, the benefits of using them can be much broader. Many of the books can be used to reinforce numbers to the youngest of children, then be reintroduced to older students as they learn the operation of addition. ELs and struggling readers can share the texts with younger students or siblings and thereby improve their literacy skills as they increase vocabulary and develop reading fluency. Also, these books can serve as models for older students as they attempt to create their own mathematical trade books. Students can analyze and discuss how different authors and illustrators work together to convey mathematical meaning and reinforce mathematical concepts.

Ehlert has written and illustrated many excellent children's books, including counting books. Often she included bright, bold illustrations that were sure to capture young readers' attention while teaching a concept. One counting book example is *Fish Eyes: A Book You Can Count On* (Ehlert, 1990), which has colorful pages that appeal to students as they count to 10. This book won several awards and was included on the IRA–CBC (Children's Book Council) Children's Choice list. Ehlert is also the illustrator for *Chicka Chicka 1, 2, 3* (Martin & Sampson, 2004), which is a sequel to the ever-popular *Chicka Chicka Boom Boom* (Martin & Archambault, 2000).

Walton's (2001) *One More Bunny: Adding From One to Ten* is another example of a counting book. When each bunny is added to the story, the reader sees the numeral, a pencil illustration for each bunny being added, and the mathematical equation. Therefore, when three little bunnies join in, there is the number 3, three drawings of bunnies, and the equation $2 + 1 = 3$. At the back of the book, Walton includes a page showing many more items that might be counted in the illustrations.

Poetry Books

Mathematical poetry books often appeal to a variety of grade levels, and it usually only takes a few minutes to read and discuss a poem. They can be shared easily, even when teachers only have a short period of time with which to work.

A number of poetry books focusing solely on math have been published in recent years, many of which include math riddles and puzzles. For example, Martin's (2003) *ABC Math Riddles* has a math riddle written for each of the 26 letters in the alphabet. Each letter is the first letter of a corresponding math term, except for the letter *X*, which is actually in the answer to the *X* riddle, *hexagon*. A variety of math terms are covered, from the easiest ones like *add* to the more difficult ones like *vertical*.

There are also a number of books, including *Arithme-Tickle: An Even Number of Odd Riddle-Rhymes* (Lewis, 2002), that contain individual math puzzles for the reader to solve and a great deal of word play. Another poetry book is Franco's (2003) *Mathematickles!*, which is actually a book of brainteasers composed from a unique combination of math and language. These brainteasers will make both students and teachers think about relationships among concepts.

Students may also enjoy the award-winning text *Marvelous Math: A Book of Poems*, edited by Hopkins (2001), which includes poems about different mathematical topics. Although *Circle-Time Poetry Math: Delightful Poems With Activities That Help Young Children Build Phonemic Awareness, Oral Language, and Early Math Skills* (Simpson, 2005) is designed for educators, it contains a number of poems about various math concepts, which will appeal to young students. Ideas for tying poetry books into mathematical poetry-writing lessons are shared in Chapter 4.

Storybooks

Mathematical storybooks are another popular type of children's literature used in the classroom. In these, there is a clear plot and storyline, which often reveal a mathematical problem. For example, in *Measuring Penny* (Leedy, 2000), the reader can follow the story of Lisa as she learns about measurement. The reader will be able to see the young girl using both standard and nonstandard units to measure Penny, her Boston terrier. After hearing the book read aloud, young students are eager to start measuring items they see in the classroom and at home. Also, teachers often enjoy using Viorst's (1978) *Alexander, Who Used to Be Rich Last Sunday* because students can follow along with the text to determine the amount of money Alexander has left from his grandparents' visit.

Another type of mathematical storybook that we see much less often deals specifically with mathematics but isn't meant to teach or reinforce a concept. One example is *Last to Finish: A Story About the Smartest Boy in Math Class* (Esham, 2008), which is about a young boy, Max, to whom many readers will be able to relate. Poor Max panics whenever the teacher requires the class to take a timed math test, resulting in peer teasing. However, near the end of the book, he finds that although problems solved through rote memorization might be difficult for him, he excels at other types of math.

Also, books like *Among the Odds & Evens: A Tale of Adventure* (Turner, 1999) may share mathematical information about odd and even numbers, but they are designed primarily as entertaining storybooks. Although books like these can be used to enhance mathematical knowledge, students need to have a firm understanding of concepts discussed in the text prior to reading these books, and teachers need to facilitate discussion to ensure that the mathematical information is understood.

Informational Books

Informational books are not normally read from cover to cover, and students often prefer to look at specific parts of these books. *G Is for Googol: A Math Alphabet Book* (Schwartz, 1998) is one example. Despite what the title may suggest, this is not a book created to enhance alphabetical knowledge. Although much of the book has information for older readers, *G Is for Googol* has pages with basic information such as *O* is for *obtuse* and *Q* is for *quantity* and *quality*. It is more than likely not a book that teachers will want to sit and read through from front to back with students. Instead it is a book that older students might enjoy if they want to read interesting information about a mathematical concept or two. Teachers may also want to share information orally about a particular term with their class. Another example is *More Math Games & Activities From*

Around the World (Zaslavsky, 2003), which is designed for ages 9 and up. Many elementary students will enjoy trying some of the activities shared within the pages.

The quality of children's literature must always be taken into consideration. Given the wide range of books available to supplement the textbook, teachers should be able to locate books that are quality literature and excellent at developing or reinforcing mathematical concepts. It is also important to always carefully look at any literature that will be incorporated into mathematics lessons to ensure that the text is appropriate.

How to Select Children's Literature for Connecting Literacy and Math

The first step in selecting children's literature is to review the available trade books. Ideally teachers can get together in groups to review and analyze books that they might want to use. By meeting with grade-level teachers to share and discuss the texts, teachers can easily understand other perspectives on books and develop ideas for the implementation of the texts in the classroom. If teachers of different grade levels can collaborate, it is even more beneficial, allowing teachers to see how skills are developed and expanded across the grades. Knowing where the skills and concepts of one grade level fit in with what is expected of students in future years and understanding the concepts that have been previously introduced by other teachers is vital to effective teaching.

Although NCTM has content and process standards detailing what students should be able to do in prekindergarten through grade 12, the council also has six principles for governing school mathematics: equity, curriculum, teaching, learning, assessment, and technology. The principle of curriculum concerns the need to have a well-articulated curricular plan across the grade levels. Reviewing children's literature that can enhance math lessons is an excellent way to do just that.

All children's literature is not created equal, and teachers cannot assume that textbook publishers have evaluated the trade books they recommend. Research shows that not all of the trade books recommended by textbook publishers are highly rated (Hunsader, 2004). When selecting literature, we have to consider the text, the context within which it will be used, and the students who will be engaged with it.

A Good Starting Point: Looking to Award Winners and Booklist Selections

It is important to select excellent texts to incorporate into lessons. Many teachers pay particular attention to the yearly Caldecott Medal and Newbery Medal winners. These medals are given for quality of illustrations and writing. However, it is necessary to look beyond award winners to find outstanding mathematical texts. By only looking at award winners, we limit our options, and we must remember that booklists are not necessarily comprised of books with the same qualities that make valuable children's literature selections.

Many content areas have their own awards and booklists. The Notable Children's Trade Books in the Field of Social Studies is a booklist compiled by the National Council for the Social Studies and the CBC. The books selected are considered to be quality books that educators can incorporate into their social studies curriculum. Then there is the Outstanding Science Trade Books for Students K–12 awards given by the National Science Teachers Association and the CBC. Although no award is given specifically to a mathematical trade book, there are other awards that teachers might review when searching for new texts to incorporate in their classrooms.

In conjunction with the CBC, IRA annually produces the Teachers' Choices and Children's Choices booklists. The Children's Choices are favorite books chosen each year by approximately 10,000 schoolchildren ages 5–13. Annotated lists for grades K–2, 3–4, and 5–6 appear each October in the journal *The Reading Teacher*. Likewise the Teachers' Choices are chosen each year by teachers, reading specialists, and librarians, and an annotated list, divided into primary, intermediate, and advanced levels, appears in the November issue of *The Reading Teacher*. (Both booklists are available online at www.reading.org/resources/booklists.aspx.)

Teachers are much more apt to find recent mathematical trade books on those lists than on others that focus solely on illustrations and content. In fact, *How Big Is It? A Big Book All About BIGness* (Hillman, 2007) and Christelow's (2007) *Five Little Monkeys Go Shopping* made the 2008 Children's Choices list. Hillman's book deals with the topic of understanding size, and Christelow's text is a simple counting book for very young children. Mathematical trade books found on these two booklists definitely should be examined for possible inclusion in the classroom because, instead of being selected by a committee as quality literature, the winners are voted on by professionals in the field and students in the classrooms.

Another award that may be worth reviewing is the Teachers' Choice Award for the Classroom given by *Learning Magazine*. Classroom teachers analyze educational products based on quality, instructional value, ease of use, and innovation to select the books for this award. *Math Poetry: Linking Language and Math in a Fresh Way* (Franco, 2006), *One Odd Day* (Fisher & Sneed, 2006), and *My Even Day* (Fisher & Sneed, 2007) are among those that have recently won this award.

Looking at IRA's Teachers' Choices and Children's Choices booklists in *The Reading Teacher* and *Learning Magazine*'s Teachers' Choice Award for the Classroom may be a good place to start. After all, books that appeal to students and teachers may be the most informative of all. However, keep in mind that these booklists and award winners include many books that are not math related, so you will likely need to expand your search to find a wide variety of quality mathematical trade books.

Using Mathematical Criteria for Selecting Children's Literature

An effective method for assessing children's literature to determine their quality and appropriateness for inclusion in your classroom instruction was designed by Schiro (1997) and revised by Hunsader (2004). This method comprises a series of criteria for evaluating books. Since mathematical trade books should be evaluated for both mathematical content and quality of literature, criteria for each are included. The reality is that no book will be perfect, and it is unrealistic to expect every trade book to be rated exceptional on each criterion. Therefore, it is important to have these six mathematical criteria to guide the selection of the best possible books for sharing in the classroom, as discussed in the following sections.

1. Is the Book's Mathematical Content Correct and Accurate? When considering a book to enhance content area learning, judging whether the mathematical content (i.e., text, computation, scale, vocabulary, and graphics) is correct and accurate is one of the most important criterion. Children's mathematical trade books can cover anything from the most basic mathematical concepts to extremely complex ones. Just as we have all heard warnings that some children's books pertaining to social studies and science may not be factually accurate, that may also be true of children's literature meant to develop mathematical concepts. With children's literature pertaining to other content areas, the teacher can often find the authors' credentials listed in the book. Sometimes the authors mention others who have served as consultants for the factual information, but this appears to occur less often with math texts. However, some publishers are eager to prove to the reader that the information in the text is correct and has been verified by listing such information on the inside cover and in the front matter.

For example, on the inside covers of *One Odd Day* (Fisher & Sneed, 2006), its sequel, *My Even Day* (Fisher & Sneed, 2007), and *Sort It Out!* (Mariconda, 2008), the reader is informed that the material was checked for accuracy by a recipient of a presidential award for mathematics, an award that varies from state to state. Although having information checked for accuracy by an outside source may be less important for mathematical books for the very young because the concepts are basic, the readers know that the publishers are making the effort to ensure that the information is presented in a clear and accurate manner.

Math Dictionary: The Easy, Simple, Fun Guide to Help Math Phobics Become Math Lovers (Monroe, 2006) is a reference book designed for older students, parents, and teachers, but it also contains interesting facts that younger students might enjoy. The inside pages provide the author's biographical information to inform the readers that the author is a professor of mathematics education, and the author acknowledges others in the field who reviewed the content for accuracy.

Although some mathematical trade books are checked for accuracy, teachers should read all children's literature with a discriminating eye. If there are doubts about any of the text's content, then double-check or share your views with colleagues before introducing the text to students.

2. Is the Book's Mathematical Content Visible and Effectively Presented?

When using quality literature, we obviously hope to instill a love of literature. With mathematical trade books, we have an additional goal of ensuring that the mathematical content is clearly part of the text. Although there are many great books that claim to develop or reinforce mathematical concepts, these concepts are not always an integral part of these texts.

The goals of the lesson must be considered. Is the book being used to introduce a concept or merely reinforce material that the students have already learned? The answer will determine whether a particular book should be used, or even when it might be best to use it, in the classroom. An excellent book for reinforcing a concept may not be appropriate at a certain time because the students are not yet familiar enough with the topic; however, the book may be perfect for complementing a lesson later on in the year. Another important question is, will the students be able to gain information or learn from the text? If there are only vague references to concepts or the illustrations confuse the reader, then it may be better to select a different book.

3. Is the Book's Mathematical Content Intellectually and Developmentally Appropriate for the Audience?
To determine this, think about the students' ages and ability levels. What mathematical concepts are appropriate for the ages and ability levels present in the classroom? Although some books are appropriate for very young students, other books are designed to be used with older readers and may contain content that is too difficult for the younger students to understand. However, even though some books may not be appropriate when they are first critiqued, the teacher may want to make note of them for sharing later in the year after the students have more hands-on experiences with a mathematical concept.

Of course, there are truly outstanding books that can appeal to and be read by a variety of ability levels. Students enjoy those books and often can reread them later to get an even richer understanding from the text. Reading texts that are potentially too challenging does not always lead to frustration for the reader: If the teacher is sharing the book and facilitating an understanding of its content, then a book on the students' instructional level is fine. However, if the students are expected to read the book and comprehend it on their own, an independent reading level is required. With the enormous number of mathematical trade books available, teachers can find plenty that appropriately challenge students and instill a love of literature.

4. Does the Book Facilitate the Reader's Involvement in, and Use and Transfer of, the Mathematics?
Although there is a time and place

for quality books that are relaxing and enjoyable solely for the aesthetic experience, books incorporated into the mathematical lessons should do more. Students should be motivated and eager to participate in the math described in the book. When it is finished, do the students want to look at it again? Do they want to learn more about the mathematical concepts discussed in the text? This is the type of involvement that should be generated by using mathematical trade books in the classroom.

5. Do the Book's Mathematics and Story Complement Each Other?
Unfortunately, there are children's books that are dull and read like a textbook, typically because the author tried to create a story simply to go with a concept. It is an artificial merging, and something about the book just does not work. Then there are the books where it appears the mathematical concepts are merely shoved in as afterthoughts, so that the students hear some facts, instead of being woven into a story line. Avoid these books and instead find ones in which the mathematical concepts and the story being told in the literature come together naturally. When the reader finishes reading or listening to the text, it should be evident that both the story line and the mathematical concepts are integral to the actual text.

6. How Great Are the Resources Needed to Help Readers Benefit From the Book's Mathematics? Instructional feasibility is always an important consideration. Books need to be easily integrated into the lessons taught. If an inordinate amount of time or expense must be spent in obtaining the materials to complete an activity in the book, then choose another text. Many books require little or no extra materials to show the reader how math appears in everyday situations and the world. Those are the type of books that students can enjoy over and over again. Think about the end goal. If the work required to effectively use the book with students is beyond the value of the results, then find another text. There are many quality children's books written that do not require excessive time and money to implement in the classroom.

Using Literary Criteria to Select Children's Literature
Along with mathematical criteria, the books have to be assessed for literary criteria. The six criteria outlined in the sections that follow are part of

Hunsader's (2004) instrument and can be used in conjunction with the mathematical criteria to select children's literature that can be effective in connecting mathematics and literacy instruction.

Some trade books may meet math criteria, but they may not be of high literary value. That does not mean that those texts should not be used to make the literacy–mathematics connection. The role of the teacher is pivotal. We must take into account students' interests and experiences and how the book will be used in the classroom. As educators, we must decide whether a book's strengths outweigh its weaknesses.

1. Does the Plot Exhibit Good Development, Imagination, and Continuity? Are the Characters (if Any) Well Developed? Even though examining the plot and characters is important, this may not apply to some mathematical books. Concept, reference, and poetry books often have no plot, so this question is not always relevant. If there is a story line, quality literature is expected to have well-developed characters, so the reader understands the characters' thoughts and feelings. Well-developed characters are in sharp contrast to flat characters, who remain the same throughout the book and have less-developed personalities. However, a characteristic of traditional literature and tales passed down orally through generations is flat characters, yet these tales are loved by children and have a lot of literary value. Therefore, analyze the children's books considered for mathematical lessons in the same meticulous manner that you scrutinize texts for use during any other time of day. Examine the characters, setting, and plot.

2. Does the Book Contain a Vivid and Interesting Writing Style That Actively Involves the Reader? Authors all have unique writing styles. Style refers to the author's word choice and the manner in which an author writes. Author style is often the reason why readers want to read more books written by an author or become hooked on a certain series of books. Teachers should read the text to determine if the type of writing in the book will engage students. If the book does not make the teacher want to read more, the writing probably won't create an interest in the students to become involved with the text. It is hard to motivate students with a book that the teacher doesn't enjoy reading. Students are intelligent and know right away if the teacher is trying to sell them on a book that the teacher doesn't like. Since the goal is to build positive attitudes and experiences with books and mathematics, teachers should use texts that they truly believe are worthwhile.

3. Are the Book's Illustrations and Graphics Relevant to the Text, Appealing, and Representative of the Students' Perspective? The illustrations and graphics can be the perfect complement for the text, although if the goal is to teach very basic math concepts, expect the illustrations to be simple. The illustrations and photographs shouldn't be confusing, and the pictures should represent items with which students are familiar. Assess the books to determine if the graphics are visually appealing. That doesn't necessarily mean that the pictures in a text have to be bright and bold. Although Ehlert has created amazing children's books with basic, vibrant pages, many students have fallen in love with Viorst's books, which contain simple black-and-white illustrations. The important thing to determine is whether the illustrations will catch the students' interest.

4. Are the Book's Readability and Interest Level Developmentally Appropriate for the Intended Audience? Readability is more than just an analysis of sentence length and word difficulty. Look at the text to determine if the students in the classroom are at the appropriate level to grasp what is written in the text. If difficult words are presented, will the context and illustrations help explain them? Are there ways the teacher can scaffold learning to make the readability level appropriate for the students? Is the content something with which the students will be interested? There are so many books available that it is possible to find ones on a variety of levels that deal with a number of topics so that all students can be exposed to texts that are at their instructional level and contain content with which they are interested.

5. Do the Book's Plot, Style, and Graphics and Illustrations Complement Each Other? This again will require professional judgment. How well does everything go together? This requires the teacher to look at the total picture.

6. Does the Book Respect the Reader by Presenting Positive Ethical and Cultural Values? This is an extremely important criterion. Children's books transmit cultural and ethical values. Are the values shown in the books ones that should be encouraged in the students with whom the book is being shared? Are there stereotypes in the illustrations or content? Do the books present a positive image of the elderly, gender roles, diverse ethnicities, and people who are different from the readers? Educators and researchers support the importance of exposing students to multiethnic literature (Altieri, 1996; Bishop, 1992; Norton, 1990) and texts portraying those who learn differently (Altieri, 2008; Andrews, 1998; Favazza & Odom, 1997). Standards 1 and 9 of the English language arts (IRA & NCTE, 1996; see Appendix A) stress the importance of students developing an understanding and respect for cultures found within the United States and around the world. Carefully selected mathematical trade books can help achieve this.

Selecting children's literature is not easy. No book will be perfect, and few will excel in every area. By using the criteria previously discussed to assess children's books, teachers can ensure that quality books infused with mathematics are selected. Think about how the texts will be used in the classroom when evaluating them. Some criteria may need to be weighted more heavily than others to determine whether the texts are acceptable for classroom use. Without discussion of texts' content in the classroom, I do not believe we can afford to share books with inaccurate mathematical information or ones that present negative images of others. Those are not books we would want to put in a classroom library or use in a listening center. It is important to remember that there is a degree of subjectivity associated with the criteria. As we all know from sharing books with teachers and students, sometimes books appeal to some people while other people find the same text less enjoyable.

Appendix C is an annotated bibliography of recently published mathematical trade books. All of the texts have been published since 2005, and some are award winners. I feel these books are excellent to include in the classroom and can each be used to help develop understanding of NCTM's Content Standards. However, as stated above, quality is always a term to which there is some subjectivity attached. The purpose of the bibliography is to present suggested books that teachers might enjoy reviewing. Take the time to look at some of the texts discussed in Appendix C and share them with colleagues.

Using Other Forms of Print Media

There are other types of print media that can be used to enhance and connect mathematical concepts. Print that is brought into the classroom context but created elsewhere is called imported text (Maloch et al., 2004). Along with actual books, many teachers enjoy incorporating print found in homes and the community. These other materials help students understand how mathematical concepts are important in texts that are part of their daily lives. This might involve incorporating menus, catalogs, magazines, newspapers, brochures, and other forms of print into lessons.

Another type of text that can be used to facilitate mathematical and literacy learning is local text, which is any text created by the teachers or students in the classroom (Maloch et al., 2004). Many students seem to have a natural interest in material they've authored. These texts are not merely handouts that a teacher might photocopy from a resource book for students—they are actually created within the walls of the classroom. Through the use of local texts, students realize that what they write and read has value. Some local texts are shared with the entire class, whereas other texts, like journal entries, are often meant for their eyes only. Both types of local text are relevant and should be considered important materials in the classroom.

Local texts provide students with a sense of ownership and pride because students are involved in their creation. This type of text affords them the opportunity to realize that they are contributing members of the classroom community and their ideas are valued. We humanize famous children's authors so that students can relate to them, but that issue doesn't occur with texts they create. They know that if other students can create books, so can they.

Creating local texts reinforces literacy skills. Students realize that they must make their thoughts clear if others are to understand the information or message being conveyed. Also, it is often easier to motivate students to reread text that they have written themselves. Mathematical local text reinforces that print has meaning and that the value of the experience lies in the ability to communicate mathematical thoughts.

Furthermore, students are enthusiastic about the material. They enjoy reading this type of print media because they have a personal association with the author. Although there are students who can't wait to show classroom visitors a mathematical trade book they are reading, student-created mathematical texts seem to draw even more excitement. If visitors come into the classroom, students are often eager to share the local texts they helped create.

Finally, these texts encourage social interaction. Our goal as educators is to create a community of learners. It is vital for students to interact with others and learn to hear and express divergent points of view. A great deal of learning occurs as others in the classroom environment share their prior knowledge and scaffold the understanding that takes place. In order for students to develop the greatest amount of mathematical knowledge or literacy skills, this social interaction is vital.

Types of Local Text

The types of local texts that might be used to make the literacy–mathematics connection will vary greatly. Local texts can include anything from mathematical word walls, which help to reinforce new mathematical concepts that students are developing, to charts that students create to show how many inches their plants grew during a certain time period. It can even include a time line the class creates to show the passage of time in a story. In addition, many teachers enjoy having their students create mathematical storybooks that can be read over and over again.

Determining Which Local Texts to Use

Similar to children's books, we must consider the quality of local text. Their value may even change over time. Maloch, Hoffman, and Patterson (2004) established the following guidelines for using local texts:

- Read your room
- Read other rooms
- Think locally
- Think relationally
- Think across the curriculum
- Think dynamically
- Create space and design

These guidelines should be considered when selecting mathematical local texts. By taking the time to "read" your room, you are looking at the types of local text you already have available for students. Think about the types of mathematical print that have been created in the classroom. If it is a public local text, how is it used in the classroom? Is it displayed where students can see it and have access to it? Then read other rooms. Some of the best ideas come from colleagues. Visit other classrooms and talk with the teachers and students. Look around at the walls, desks, and work areas to see what types of local text you may want to add to your own room. Likewise, invite other teachers into your classroom. Through collaboration, you can improve the quality and quantity of mathematical local text that you have available.

The following list includes some ideas that you might want to consider when reading the local mathematical texts in your classroom:

- Have the students been engaged with the local text in the classroom recently? If not, is there a way to draw their attention to it again to further learning, or is it time to replace the text?
- Does the public local text displayed include examples created by various students in the classroom so that all of the students feel ownership?
- Is local text integrated throughout the room and not just in a math center or one part of the classroom, so students can realize that math is important throughout the curriculum?
- Were students able to weave their experiences and knowledge from outside the classroom into the local text created?

According to Maloch and colleagues (2004), "One critical benefit of the use of local texts in classrooms is the opportunity they provide to reach beyond the classroom walls" (p. 155).

Now that you have assessed the strengths and weaknesses of the local texts you have available, think about the mathematical concepts currently being taught and those that will be taught in the future. Are there additional ways that local texts can be created from the different experiences? Plan ahead to find ways that you can integrate more local texts into the classroom. Also, think relationally. Maloch and colleagues (2004) suggest that teachers think about how they can create a personal text for public texts that are created and vice versa. If students create a large chart about geometric concepts that they are learning, the students might then make a personal text, such as a journal entry, about one geometric concept that they see at home or in the community. Likewise, if students illustrate story problems on a sheet of paper, they might later select one of the problems from their paper to go into a student-created book for the classroom library. We don't have to limit ourselves to thinking solely about mathematics. Local texts that tie into mathematics might further enhance learning across the curriculum. Often, student-created time lines can be connected to both mathematics and social studies learning, and charts might also pertain to a variety of content areas.

The final two guidelines, think dynamically and create space and design, both deal with the classroom environment. Think dynamically is probably one of the most important guidelines. Just as you wouldn't want to keep all of the imported texts in your classroom long after the interest is gone, you need to change your local texts on a regular basis. Even after working with students to create local texts that seem perfect, as time passes the greatest creations get tiring and old. When students are no longer engaged with mathematical charts, diagrams, and other local texts, it is time to replace or modify them. Fortunately, local texts are so easily woven into lessons that they can be changed frequently. As you modify and change the local texts, think about the space and design of your classroom. There is a difference between a print-rich environment and one that is messy. The key is the fine line that exists between the two environments.

See Table 1 for a list of the different types of imported and local texts that can be used. The list is not all inclusive, but it does provide examples that should generate even more ideas when shared with colleagues. Although all of the texts may be found in many classrooms, the key is that the texts listed might easily be used to support the literacy–mathematics connection. Although texts are either imported or local, depending on their origin, the list is not broken down into two distinct groups. If students create recipes within a classroom, then the texts are local, whereas a cookbook from home is an imported text. The quality and usage of the text in the classroom is important. Although it is great to have many of the texts on the list in a classroom, the type of interaction the students have with

Table 1. Types of Imported and Local Texts for Building the Literacy–Mathematics Connection

Books (student-created, trade, and text)	Graphs	Recipes
	Journal entries	Textbooks
Calendars	Learning center activities	Time lines
Catalogs	Magazines	Travel brochures
Charts	Maps	Wall charts
Diagrams	Menus	Word walls
Flash cards	Newspapers	Worksheets
Games	Number lines	
Graphic organizers	Posters and other visuals	

them is even more important. However, this list is a good starting point for teachers to use when examining their classrooms.

WHERE DO I GO FROM HERE?

In this chapter, a variety of texts that might be integrated through literacy and mathematics instruction have been discussed. We read for meaning, and these texts reinforce the message that print has meaning. They also help students gain mathematical knowledge. By incorporating diverse materials into our classrooms, we provide rich experiences for the students to understand that literacy and math are not two discrete compartmentalized times of the day, but instead are interwoven aspects of the curriculum that are equally important to us.

As we move on in this book, you will see that there are many different ways to enhance literacy knowledge while fostering the development of mathematical skills. It is important to remember that the print available in the classroom is the foundation. No longer is it necessary to rely solely or even heavily upon the mathematics textbook. By providing a variety of texts, both imported and local, we enrich mathematical lessons. Well-planned use of the texts will enable students to understand that their classroom learning connects across content areas and outside the classroom into their homes and communities. These texts will help remove the barrier that exists between literacy and mathematics and reinforce the belief that learning itself cannot be compartmentalized. Learning is ongoing and continuous. By making classroom learning relevant to the world, we provide students with the literacy and mathematical skills they need not only to function but also to be successful in the world.

PART II

The Connection in Action: Improving Mathematical Skills While Fostering Literacy Growth

CHAPTER 3

Strengthening Writing Skills While Communicating Mathematical Knowledge

The process of writing is as important as the finished product. Students need to take the time to slowly progress through the stages of writing in order to become better writers. They need to make mistakes, reflect on those errors, and then write some more. Like many things in life, writing isn't a skill that can be explained, quickly comprehended, and then the desired results achieved. Writing has to be experienced.

Writing is a topic that has been examined by researchers for years and continues to be explored. Many of the major researchers and theorists have looked at how writing skills develop (Dyson, 2006; Graves, 1991; Strickland & Morrow, 1988). All of the research pointed to one key fact: Students learn to write by writing (Graves, 1983). Even though this concept is known, it is often tempting to shorten classroom writing time by providing writing prompts, fill-in-the-blank exercises, and workbooks. However, if we truly want our students to become writers, we must move beyond these rote activities and instead provide authentic, engaging, and meaningful writing activities. By connecting writing with content areas such as mathematics, we not only make writing relevant but also make better use of our limited instructional time. Students are able to improve both mathematics and writing skills simultaneously.

The power of integrating writing throughout the mathematics curriculum is not a new discovery. The educational field realized the importance in the 1980s when a great deal was published about writing across the curriculum (Pugalee, 1997). Today one would expect that writing would be a fairly common fixture in the mathematics curriculum. However, a survey conducted with teachers in New York who were NCTM members revealed that the majority of them either did not use writing in mathematics classes or were unfamiliar with how to use it (Silver, 1999). Many teachers are aware of the advantages of writing throughout the curriculum and understand the importance of developing students' writing skills while helping them improve and deepen their mathematical knowledge; however, integrated writing is still not a common practice in schools today.

Writing is an important component of the English language arts standards. Standards 4, 5, and 12 (IRA & NCTE, 1996; see Appendix A) specifically mention the importance of students using written language for a variety of purposes and for different audiences. Likewise, NCTM's (2000) Communication Standard (see Appendix B) states that students must be able to communicate their mathematical thinking to others. Connecting writing and mathematics is a natural way to help accomplish this.

The goal of this chapter is to help educators create and maintain the writing–mathematics connection. We begin by helping students understand that they have something important to say and helping them learn how to get their initial thoughts on paper, which is often the most difficult part of writing. From there, we discuss how to maintain a strong connection so that students continue to be engaged in mathematical writing. That part of the chapter includes a variety of activities that can help students maintain the connection through more formal writing. The activities include both creative and informative writing and provide additional opportunities for students to see that writing and mathematics have an important connection. Through the ideas presented, educators can help students develop a sense of audience and purpose while reinforcing their mathematical knowledge.

Getting Mathematical Ideas on Paper

When asking students to write, teachers often hear a student respond, "I don't have anything to talk about." Many students experience writer's block—they cannot think of anything to write. However, once students get started and realize that they can be successful, they are more apt to want to continue writing. Fortunately, when we ask our students to write about recent mathematical learning, we are providing them with a relevant topic, which can make this process easier. Therefore, some of the stress surrounding writing is removed, and students realize they have something valuable to share.

We can spark students' interest and help them see how mathematics and literacy are connected through these three activities: quick-writes, mathematical journals, and admit/exit slips. Although these activities do not take much more time than would be required for students to complete writing prompts or worksheets, these activities have a much greater value. They can all be modified in consideration of the individual learners, goals of the lesson, and the classroom context. They provide the teacher with the opportunity to tailor the writing assignment to the individual lesson or topic. Also, real-life writing rarely involves completing writing prompts or filling out worksheets; therefore, to make literacy connections more relevant and prepare students to function in the world as literate individuals, we must provide these experiences.

Teachers can modify each of the activities to meet their needs and the needs of their students. Through these activities, teachers can see quickly the background knowledge that students bring to the lesson, understand the connections that students make with mathematical content, realize where students may struggle with a mathematical concept and need reinforcement, and even confirm growth in mathematical knowledge. Students can also make connections between the mathematical information they gained and the world around them. Furthermore, they are able to reinforce any learning by reflecting on the topics, forming their thoughts into words, and getting those ideas on paper. During all of this, students gain more experience writing and therefore become more self-confident in their ability to write.

Quick-Writes

The quick-write is the easiest type of writing to integrate. A quick-write is exactly what the name implies—quick—but allows students to find their voice and realize that they have something to say (Rief, 2003). This type of writing naturally requires a minimal amount of instructional time. Students generally are given a limited period of time to respond to a topic, which may be as little as 60 seconds or as long as 5 minutes depending on the topic, the students' ages, and the ability levels present in the classroom.

One of the benefits of this strategy is its flexibility. Modifications to this exercise allow all students to respond to the best of their abilities. If the teacher chooses, the topic may vary on any given day, or the students may be given a few topics to choose from. Another option that adds variety is allowing students to work in groups to complete the quick-writes. The decisions guiding how the experience is structured in the classroom depends on the teacher's purpose for the activity. For instance, is the purpose to informally assess what students know about a topic, or is it to get students thinking and focused on the topic?

The quick-write strategy can be used at different times during a mathematics lesson. Teachers may use this strategy similarly to how they use a prereading strategy by asking students to complete a quick-write before introducing a new mathematical topic. When used in this manner, the quick-writes can serve as an informal assessment to determining the background knowledge the students possess on the topic. Therefore, quick-writes provide important information for planning appropriate instruction. Another benefit is that this type of writing reveals any mathematical misconceptions students have on a particular topic. After reviewing the students' quick-writes, either through an oral sharing of student responses or by the teacher reading them, the teacher can discuss any misconceptions and clarify information related to the concept.

Let's look at how quick-writes might pertain to a common topic introduced in the elementary grades: the metric system. As part of NCTM's (2000) Measurement Standard (see Appendix B), students are expected to understand both the customary system and the metric system. Teachers can introduce the metric system by reading aloud and discussing one of the excellent picture books available on the topic. For example, very young students may enjoy hearing *Polly's Pen Pal* (Murphy, 2005), in which the main character, Polly, wants to learn about the metric system to communicate with her new pen pal in Canada. Then the pen pals will be able to talk about distances, how tall they are, and how hot it is where they live.

While many students living in countries that use a system of measurement not based on the metric system may wonder why they need to learn metrics, this book quickly shows the readers that the customary system is not the only way to measure, just as students living in countries that use the metric system will realize that there are various systems of measurement in the world. Another book that serves this purpose well is *Millions to Measure* by Schwartz (2003), which explains the history of the metric system and has an appendix containing additional information.

After sharing one of these books, the teacher may choose to use a quick-write like the following:

> Before we begin learning about the metric system, write down everything you already know about the metric system. You have three minutes.

This quick-write takes a minimal amount of time and easily ties writing into the mathematics classroom. The completed quick-writes provide the teacher with information on the background knowledge that each student possesses on the topic. Students can also learn from others by sharing their quick-writes with peers. As information is discussed, scaffolding occurs, and students' schema regarding the concept can be modified to incorporate new information acquired during sharing.

Another idea is to use a quick-write to segue from a broad topic into a narrower topic. When used in this manner, quick-writes provide an excellent opportunity for the teacher to tie in prior mathematical learning to the current day's topic and narrow the focus of the writing. For instance, perhaps a teacher has already started to explain the concept of measurement, and the students have been introduced to Cleary's (2008) book *On the Scale, a Weighty Tale*. This book, with its zany illustrations and memorable rhyme, discusses everything about weight from grams to pounds to tons. The teacher may then want to narrow the topic to a specific type of measurement. If the teacher's purpose is to focus on measuring liquids, then a quick-write could be tailored more specifically to this goal with a topic, such as,

> Yesterday we started learning about measurement, and today we are going to talk about measuring liquid. Take 60 seconds to tell me the different ways you are aware of to measure liquid.

If the teacher analyzes the responses from the class to this quick-write, the feedback can guide lesson planning. The teacher knows what areas need emphasis in class and what misconceptions need clarification. The responses may even help the teacher choose minilessons geared toward students who are still struggling with basic information.

A quick-write also can be used at the end of the mathematics lesson to tie learning together and bring closure to the lesson. When used in this manner, the quick-write can serve as an excellent review for the students. By bringing closure to the lesson, students reflect on all they have learned and deepen their understanding of the topic. The following is one example of this type of quick-write:

> Take one minute to explain the difference between an acute angle, a right angle, and an obtuse angle.

This example not only requires students to summarize and explain the three types of angles but also moves students beyond comprehension-level knowledge to high-level thinking. They analyze and synthesize their knowledge to compare and contrast the angles, and they communicate their thoughts in writing to complete the quick-write.

One teacher used quick-writes for a much broader topic during a math lesson after a lengthy school break. When she asked her third graders to share what they learned so far that year in mathematics, their answer was division. She then had the class work in pairs to write down everything they knew about the topic of division. Two third-grade students worked together and came up with the following response:

> Division
> It is the opposite of multiplying.
> It is repeated subtraction.
> You can use a number line to help divide.
> You just really make equal groups.
> You can check by multiplying.
> Fact familys are the same for dividing and multiplying

It is clear from this response that these two students remembered some basic information about division. They knew how to check their answers and understood the relationship of fact families with multiplication and division. Also, they remembered hints the teacher provided during lessons, such as the ability to use a number line to guide their work. By pairing the students, they experienced cooperative learning and scaffolded each other through discussing, sharing, and reflecting on the knowledge they possessed.

To take this type of writing a step further, teachers can have students apply their new mathematical knowledge outside the classroom learning context. This allows students to not only communicate their mathematical knowledge to others but also to connect this knowledge to the world around them, which is one of the goals of the NCTM (2000) standards.

The following is one example of a quick-write that requires students to apply their knowledge outside the classroom:

Today's lesson focused on geometry and shapes. Quickly create a list of places where you might see geometric shapes on a walk around the school and neighborhood. You have two minutes.

This type of quick-write helps extend student learning beyond the classroom. The students move beyond basic recognition and labeling of shapes to applying the information to the world around them. Students may talk about concrete examples, such as the rectangular shape of a flag in front of the school or the square found in a pattern on the local grocery store sign, or more abstract examples. Students may mention that their family sits in a circle to put together a jigsaw puzzle and that the sun creates the perfect triangle of light on their bedroom window at various times during the day. Enabling students to understand the relevance of mathematics and realize that mathematics is more than just a subject in school is vital to helping students see the importance of what they are learning. Connecting literacy and math learning to the world around them is extremely important.

Even though teachers can gain a great deal of knowledge from reading quick-writes, the activity does not need to end there. If teachers choose to have students create individual quick-writes, the students might then share their writing with the rest of the class or in larger groups. One second-grade teacher regularly has her class do that. She calls it "Spill Your Brains." Often after math lessons, the students grab their math journals and "spill" onto the pages what they learned during math that day. The teacher requires the students to use a couple of new vocabulary words they learned recently. If the students are unable to write complete sentences, she modifies the task by having them illustrate their thoughts. After allowing 15 minutes to spill onto the paper what they learned during math, students are chosen at random to share their ideas with the rest of the class.

Quick-writes can be expanded beyond sharing by writing a journal entry about some of the ideas learned from classmates, or students might correct misconceptions that they initially wrote about mathematical topics.

Journal Writing

Similar to quick-writes, journal writing is an informal writing strategy, but unlike quick-writes, students are given more time to reflect on and develop their ideas. According to Nahrang and Peterson (1986), there are basically two characteristics of journaling: Students can proceed at their own pace and develop an understanding based on their own experiences. By allowing students time to think about their topic and share their ideas, a lot can be learned. When teachers choose to use short journal entries to help students reflect back on what they learned after a period of time, mathematical content is being reinforced. The teacher can extend this learning by having some of the students discuss what they wrote. This may help struggling students remember mathematical concepts and terms and better understand new content.

One second-grade teacher asked her students to write what they enjoyed learning the most that year in math. One student, Destinee, wrote the following:

> I favorite thing that I Leaned is symmetry. Becuase you get to grow lines in the metol of a shape to see if it has the same size. I like to color inside of in whin I am done.

Many young students enjoy learning about symmetry, so Destinee's response may not come as a surprise. She used her knowledge of graphophonemic relationships to help her spell the term *symmetry*, then she corrected her spelling by using the environmental print found in the math center. The more she sees and writes mathematical terms such as *symmetry*, the more apt she is to make them a part of her sight vocabulary. Her second sentence indicates that she understands the geometric concept that, if a symmetrical shape is divided in two, the sides are equal. As Destinee continues to write about mathematical concepts, she will refine her word choice to communicate her mathematical ideas more clearly.

Mathematical journal writing also serves to strengthen the relationship between students' experiences and the content knowledge they are gaining. One teacher asked fifth-grade students to think about how they used mathematics during the day. Kenya wrote the following:

> In the morning when I wake up I calcate how much time I have, to get to the bus stop. At school I add up $2.00 to buy some hot wings. When I get on the bus I have to count to make sure I have a seat to sit on.

Kenya showed that mathematics begins as soon as she gets out of bed when she has to figure out the amount of time she has to get ready for school. Her entry also reveals that she understands that money is another important mathematical concept that she uses throughout the day. Even going home at the end of the day requires math because she looks to determine if there is a seat left for her on the bus.

Students might then share their journal entries in groups, or the teacher may choose to guide the discussion by asking students to think about statements they made. For example, with a specific math topic provided, many students may mention using money during the day, and the teacher could ask them to think about the mathematical operations they use when they deal with money. If students buy hot wings for lunch, similarly to the way Kenya did, then they may have to subtract money. If another student mentions that a parent provided money in the morning to buy class pictures, the student would have to add the amount of money received to the amount already in a pocket for lunch. Through writing and the rich discussion that can ensue, students can express what mathematical knowledge they possess and refine and build on that knowledge.

Working in groups can add to the benefits gained through both quick-writes and mathematical journals. For both forms of writing, students might get in groups prior to the lesson beginning and brainstorm ideas together. A group-written entry may reveal less information about individual students' knowledge level on a topic, but will enable the students to learn from each other and hear others' ideas. The discussion can be invaluable, and the activity can help the struggling students learn from their peers. Also keep in mind that we must build ELs' oral language skills in a second language. This type of group activity helps ELs develop the vocabulary necessary to talk about a mathematical concept.

Admit/Exit Slips

Another type of informal writing well suited for establishing the literacy–mathematics connection is admit/exit slips. These slips of paper are often called either admit slips or exit slips, but some teachers use them for both purposes (Robb, 1999). After writing about a teacher-assigned idea on a slip of paper, students use the slip as their ticket out of class or into class. Many teachers I have worked with prefer to use them as exit slips, so students can reflect back on what they learned that day in school. As an exit slip, students can quickly complete it before getting ready to leave for home. Then when parents or guardians ask what the children learned that day in school, hopefully their students will be more apt to remember after having reflected and written about it at the end of the day.

Furthermore, teachers can use the information gained from the completed exit slips to plan ahead for the next day's lesson. This activity is a quick and easy way to meet a variety of teacher goals, including bringing a lesson to closure, learning about mathematical misconceptions, helping students reflect on their learning, and once again helping them articulate their mathematical knowledge through writing. Like quick-writes and journal entries, these slips can be an easy way for students to quickly share mathematical information and enable the teacher to assess individual knowledge, mathematical gains, and areas that may need further reinforcement.

Recently when I was working with a first-grade teacher, the students were asked before they went to lunch what they had learned earlier that day in math. I had to smile when a student immediately said "nothing," and another nodded his head in agreement. Obviously after half a day in school, the students had learned something, and I am sure they learned important information that their teacher wanted them to remember. The teacher took this opportunity to ask them what they did in math that day. Even though the initial responses were "nothing," it was quickly evident as the students shared their ideas that they had been very busy learning about money. Then the teacher asked each student to share in writing one thing that they learned in math that day. Through oral discussion, reflecting on the day's activities, and having the students articulate on an exit slip one thing they learned, the teacher reinforced that day's learning. The exit slip served to motivate the students to think about and assess what they had learned in math class.

Daytwana wrote this on her exit slip:

I learned hwo to cwnt penes.

Although her exit slip contains several misspelled words, the content is important. Completing the slip allowed Daytwana to look back at what she had learned, which helped her remember the content that was discussed that day and articulate the new knowledge that she had gained. Since the teacher asked for a sentence, Daytwana also put a capital letter at the beginning and a period at the end. Therefore, Daytwana was reinforcing the knowledge she had about sentences.

Daytwana's writing shows that she is continuing to develop an understanding of vowel diphthongs through the use of invented spelling and that *penny* is a relatively new term for this first grader, since it is still not part of her sight vocabulary. By continuing to analyze Daytwana's informal writing, the teacher can monitor her writing growth as well as her mathematical gains. Daytwana was excited to tell everyone that she had learned to count pennies. She even drew four pennies on the paper and wrote "four cents" next to them. The illustration drawn on her exit slip confirmed that Daytwana can count pennies.

The teacher could choose to structure the exit slip writing experience even more by asking the students to explain on the slip what they learned about pennies or when they use them. In addition, the slip could be used to explain the differences between two concepts. Students might talk about the differences between a penny and a nickel. Even though the teacher wasn't using the exit slip as a formal assessment, it is obvious that Daytwana understands how to count pennies. Plus, the open-ended exit slip allowed students to come up with a variety of responses and reiterate what they learned.

There are many additional uses for admit/exit slips. Students can write one new thing they learned that day in mathematics and why it is important to state any information from the lesson that may still be unclear. By asking these questions, the teacher develops a better understanding of what concepts need further clarification. Students too shy to announce to the entire class that they don't understand something often do not mind privately sharing the difficulty with the teacher.

If teachers prefer using the slips at the beginning of class, they can ask the students to write down one way that they used mathematics at home the night before, which enables them to see the value of mathematics outside of the classroom and make connections between mathematics and the real world. The admit/exit slips are an excellent way to help students communicate their mathematical knowledge. The activity takes a minimal amount of class time and pulls the lesson together.

The most important thing to remember is the purpose of the writing. While we want to encourage quality writing, we normally don't expect students to have final draft–quality writing in their quick-writes, journal writing, and admit/exit slips. Often teachers let parents know that perfection is not required or even expected in this type of writing. Teachers may choose to articulate this by stamping "draft" on the paper. The main goal of connecting mathematics and literacy through informal writing is to help students feel comfortable with communicating their mathematical knowledge. We are helping the students make the literacy–mathematics connection.

Strengthening Mathematical Writing Skills

As young students develop the literacy–mathematics connection through informal writing, we need to find engaging ways to keep them writing. Students in this day and age expect and thrive on variety; they want to be actively involved, and they want new challenges. By varying the purpose of writing and the audience for the text, we can help keep students interested.

As discussed in the Preface, we want students not only to function in the world around them but also to thrive. To be considered literate adults, individuals must be able to write to inform, persuade, entertain, and even raise questions. Furthermore, adults often are expected to communicate information to a variety of audiences. However, teachers are challenged with finding time to develop these complex writing skills. This type of writing is more formal and often requires a great deal of class time. By connecting students' mathematical learning with this more formal type of writing, we can help students deal with time constraints. Teachers are then strengthening the literacy–mathematics connection and helping students meet the increasing content and writing demands.

Although many people may not think of creative writing as a natural fit for math, there is no reason that students cannot be creative while reinforcing mathematical understanding. Students often enjoy the opportunity to use their imagination when writing, and therefore creative writing can help them develop positive views of mathematics. By writing about mathematical terms, even in a fictional story, students can reflect on mathematical content. They also can reinforce their knowledge of the story structure found in fictional stories. Writing roulette and creative stories are two ways students can make the literacy–mathematics connection through fictional writing.

Writing Roulette

Writing roulette is always a lot of fun for students, and I use it often with older students. Teachers begin by reviewing the parts of a story with the class. Stories of all kinds typically have an introduction, middle, and conclusion, and as a class the students brainstorm what they might expect to find in each section of a story. Typically in the introduction, the reader is exposed to the characters, the setting (i.e., time and place), and the conflict central to the story. The plot then develops in the story's middle section, which may even end with the story's climax. The text leading up to the climax builds suspense and makes the reader want to read the last section to find some type of resolution.

After reviewing the parts of a story, teachers should provide a list of mathematical terms that the class has learned or let the students brainstorm a class list. The students orally read through the list, and the teacher ensures that the math terms are familiar by clarifying their meanings with students. The teacher then explains the purpose of the assignment. The students will create fictional stories, incorporating a variety of math terms. This is an excellent time to share a few mathematical storybooks that use math terms in the story line as models. Older students may enjoy reading the tale of Sir Cumference, his wife Lady Di of Ameter, and their son Radius in *Sir Cumference and the First Round Table: A Math Adventure* (Neuschwander, 1999). Younger students can likewise enjoy the adventures of the triangle in *The Greedy Triangle* (Burns, 2008).

Finally, it is time for the writing to begin. Students break up into groups of three, then each student in the class writes an introduction to a story incorporating some of the mathematical terms on the brainstormed list. The teacher decides whether to require a certain number of terms or let the individual students determine how many to use. I prefer to require a minimum number of terms be included in each part of the story that students will write. Since other students will read the story parts, students must keep their handwriting as neat as possible. Allowing the students to type the stories on class computers is a great idea if the classroom has computers or if a computer lab is available.

The teacher stops the students after a specified period of time, which will vary depending on the levels and ages of the students. I often gauge the amount of time by monitoring the students, so I can tell when the majority are finished writing their introductions. I then tell students that they have a couple minutes remaining before they must stop writing. I remind them at that time that they should have introduced the conflict, the characters, and the setting to the reader.

Then each student exchanges papers with someone else in their group or moves to another group member's computer. At this point, all students are looking at an introduction they did not write. The students read through what was written and write the middle section of the new story. Once again, students are reminded that they should attempt to incorporate some of the mathematical terms and that they do not want to bring the story to closure at this point, as they are merely detailing the plot. Although the activity involves using the math terms, the story still needs to make sense. The terms shouldn't just be listed or mentioned but actually woven into the story line.

After a period of time, all students stop writing. The students in each group exchange their stories with the person in the group who has not previously contributed to that story. Therefore, each member of a three-person group contributes to each of the stories in their group. The students now write the conclusions to the mathematical stories. The amount of time given for writing needs to increase each time the stories are exchanged because students need an adequate amount of time to read and think about what has already been written in the story.

One sixth-grade language arts class brainstormed a list of 30 math terms. The teacher then divided her class into groups of three, and each group created a writing roulette story incorporating some of the terms. Three students created an interesting story regarding a math class and its fictitious teacher, Mrs. Jinkins:

> Attention Class, said Mrs. Jinkins. The whole class jumped. Mrs. Jinkins slaped the yard stick on the desk and said NOW. We were now paying close attention to the board. She said, Jonny what is the quotient of 24 divided into 136,727. My heart was racing. I didn't know the answer. I quickly tried to do it on my paper. She said What is the answer. Don't you know? I said "NO." She said sharply, see me after class. The girls in the corner giggled. Including Sally. She is my crush.
>
> My face turned bright red. I was waiting for her to stop, which took what felt like ten minutes. During class, while Mrs. Jinkins was teaching us about exponents,

fractions, and division, I kept trying to answer the problem on a scrap piece of paper. Finally, I got the answer. I raised my hand. Mrs. Jinkins answered "what" in a really rude tone. The answer to the problem is 5696. Mrs. Jinkins looked at me like I was crazy. The answer to 3 to the fourth power is not 5,696. I explained to her about the answer she had asked me at the beginning of class. She finally remembered and looked surprised. Mrs. Jenkins checked in her math book to see if I was right. She looked at me with great enthusiam. It was amost like she was the happiest and most proud that she had ever been.

Mrs. Jenkins said, "Jonny you are apselutly correct.

My heart jumped out of my chest. During that following day we went to recess after math class. I was hanging with all my playing basket ball. Then all of a sudden I hear a young lady calling. "Johny! Jonny!" Over at the bushes on the opposite side of the basket ball court.

I turned my head and there was beuatifull Sally. I horridly rushed towards her. When I finally got there she teasing me about the math problem. I laughed along.

"You were suly good finding the quotient" she said. We talked more about math and out of no where she asked if I could go with her. Then she kissed me on my cheek and ran away. My face turned red.

I was very excited.

The three students tied the story and mathematical terms to their own interests and experiences as adolescents. In this example, the students used dialogue, even though they are still developing an understanding of quotation marks. These students demonstrated a firm grasp of story structure, from the introduction to the conclusion.

Teachers may choose to use the stories created by the class to help determine minilessons that target specific writing skills that need to be refined. Perhaps students can be directed to think about their use of vivid adjectives or powerful verbs. Teachers could also choose excerpts from the stories created that serve as excellent examples of different literacy concepts to share with the students. This type of writing lends itself well to process writing; the class may proceed from the rough draft through to the final editing stages of their papers. Students can then compile the stories into a book to be used in the classroom or taken home to share with their families.

The writing roulette activity is a great way to engage students in creating a story. Even though many enjoy the writing strategy because they use their imaginations, the students also do an excellent job of incorporating some of their math terms. Many students are surprised at the amount of text they write through the process, since they typically would not write a story individually that is as long as one created through writing roulette. I like to point out to students that it is much easier to create a detailed story with this strategy because they are building on each other's stories and ideas.

Writing roulette is an easy way to incorporate mathematical writing into the classroom. Students find it an enjoyable activity and like to see how other students expand stories and perhaps add some unexpected twists to the original plot.

Creative Stories

Elementary students also enjoy creating fictitious stories that explain certain mathematical concepts. As with writing roulette, the teacher may choose to read a mathematical story book to the class in which certain words are tied into the story line. This book can serve as a model (or mentor) text for the story the students write themselves. Students may work in groups to create the stories, but unlike writing roulette, the group is responsible for writing the entire story together. Also, the goal is to explain a mathematical concept in depth. Instead of tying a variety of mathematical terms into a narrative, the students focus on explaining one mathematical concept, which may be selected by the teacher or the students.

One sixth-grade class was allowed to choose the term for their story and work in pairs or small groups. Two students created the following story about cubing and a magic number:

> Cubed: Three is a Magic Number
>
> There once was a cubed symbol who was stubborn, stubborn, stubborn. Then he met a Genie that gave him three, three, three wishes. He wished to have a friend to understand, stand, stand him. He wished he was the most important symbol of all, all, all. His last wish was to live a happy life forever, ever, ever.

The brief story was a great opportunity for the students to experience creative writing about a mathematical concept. Although the teacher allowed the students the freedom to create any type of story, this group of students incorporated many elements of folktales into the short story they authored. The story begins similarly to many others that begin with "once upon a time." There are three wishes granted to the main character, the cube character is flat in that not a lot of details are revealed about it, and the story ends with the cube living happily ever after. These two students obviously understood the concept of cubing by the title of the story and the repetition of using words three times in a row. Similar to how many picture books state a theme or a lesson to be learned inside the book, the students wrote inside the front page: "Cubed—the product in which a number is a factor three times."

Creative stories also provide an excellent opportunity for students to share with a younger audience. Teachers can facilitate this type of learning experience by talking with teachers in the younger grades about the specific mathematical concepts being introduced to the younger students as well as any areas that could use additional reinforcement. Then the older students work in groups to brainstorm and develop creative stories that reinforce those concepts through the text and illustrations. The older students feel the pride of authorship and experience sharing something they wrote with a real audience. Younger students benefit from the experience by having mathematical concepts reinforced and seeing older students enjoying the topic of mathematics. This activity can create positive attitudes toward writing and math.

Writing to Inform

As adults, most of our writing is informational. We often find ourselves drafting business e-mails, letters, reports, and the like to share information with the recipients. Therefore, it is important that students learn to write informational pieces. By developing this form of writing, we expand the range of ways students can write. Through informative writing, they develop the ability to describe concepts clearly and concisely.

In this section, two types of writing that encourage informational writing are described: pen pal letters and cubing, a specific writing strategy whose origin is credited to Neeld (Neeld & Kiefer, 1990). Although some educators may use these methods for other purposes in their classrooms, the intent here is to share how these two strategies can be used to strengthen the literacy–mathematics connection while refining students' informational writing skills.

Pen Pals

Pen pal letter writing can be facilitated by having students write to students in different classrooms, grade levels, or even communities. Another possibility is to arrange pen pal relationships between students and adults in the community. Many students enjoy writing and receiving letters, and this activity has been successful with special-education students (Rankin, 1992).

Thanks to modern technology, many teachers choose to have students communicate with others via e-mail. Mathematical pen pals can be maintained with those outside the immediate area via the Internet. When using the Internet, pen pals can be located in a different state or even a different country. Even though a get-together is unlikely across such distances, students often enjoy learning about a new area and a new way of life. As discussed previously in this chapter, if the pen pals live in a different country, the metric system may be an excellent place to begin conversations.

Students love to talk to their peers, and pen pal letters and e-mails can encourage students to talk about their mathematical understanding. If teachers opt for pen pals from other grades, younger students can write about what they are learning in school and more specifically communicate what they are learning in math to the older students. This requires both students to reflect on their learning to articulate and summarize the mathematical concepts. It also encourages students to discuss mathematical ideas, problems, and opinions with students in other grades.

Younger students might work as a class to create questions for the older students to answer in their responses. This provides a great opportunity to reinforce mathematical learning beyond the classroom walls. If younger students are being introduced to multiplication, they can ask the older students how they use multiplication in their lives and why they think it is important to learn. Both groups of pen pals benefit from the experience. The younger students must effectively communicate their mathematical ideas, and the older students develop an understanding of how to explain their answers and reasoning. Both groups must think about mathematics in new ways.

Teachers should continue the pen pal correspondence on a consistent basis throughout the year to maintain interest in the letters and e-mails. Many students are eager to get a response from their pen pals. If the pen pals are in the same school or community, the teachers may arrange a pen pal get-together at the end of the year. The older students or community members can meet the younger students for refreshments or read an age-appropriate mathematical trade book to their pen pals.

All of the students benefit from the pen pal gathering. Even if some of the older students are struggling readers, the experience still enhances their literacy skills. By reading and rereading a picture book to share with younger students, the older students increase their sight word vocabulary and improve their fluency. Plus, the authentic experience provides motivation for the older students to work on improving reading skills. Because the picture books do not need to be extremely difficult, the older students can reap the benefits of developing confidence in their reading skills and enjoy the fact that the younger students view them as reading role models. The younger students also benefit by hearing and enjoying a new story.

Cubing

We encourage students to look at a topic from a variety of perspectives, but this is more easily said than done. Cubing is one type of writing that can help achieve this goal. This strategy is challenging for students, and I have found that it often takes quite a bit of classroom time to complete unless the strategy is modified.

Cubing, often used with older students (e.g., Neeld & Kiefer, 1990), was designed to help students look at a topic from different perspectives, just like the six sides of a cube. The purpose of the activity was to help with writer's block. As cubing was originally planned, students brainstormed each of the six perspectives for three to five minutes, then wrote on each of these perspectives:

1. Describe it
2. Associate it
3. Compare it
4. Analyze it
5. Apply it
6. Argue for or against it

Since many students are unfamiliar with this type of writing, I prefer using it initially for a general writing activity to ensure the students understand the expectations before they apply it to a specific content area like mathematics. Introducing this activity to the entire class and allowing students to work in groups to complete the writing works well. I have used this activity with third graders and middle-school students in a variety of settings, and the results are often impressive. When I initially use this strategy with students, I brainstorm all perspectives for a topic with an entire class. For younger students, I select a simple mathematical topic to which they can relate, such as time, the measurement system, and even specific coins or shapes. When teachers determine whether to use this strategy, they should look at each perspective to see if there are ways that students can look at a specific mathematical topic from that view.

For example, if students are studying shapes, they may choose to look at rectangles. Can they describe a rectangle (e.g., four sides, corners)? What do they associate with rectangles (e.g., mirrors, tables, the classroom floor, lights in the ceiling)? Can the students compare it to a triangle (e.g., four sides and angles versus three sides and angles)? Are the students able to analyze it in detail (e.g., right angles found where each side connects, sides parallel to each other)? Can they say when they use rectangles (e.g., a special dining room table for Sunday dinners, their desks in a rectangular shape for group work, their homes)? Can the students state whether they think rectangles are important or unimportant (e.g., A rectangular computer screen is easier to view than perhaps a screen that is circular or triangular.)?

If possible, I like to use a cube or box with each perspective listed on a different side. Looking at one side, as a class we brainstorm a list of words the students think of when they hear that perspective, and I jot those ideas down on a sheet of paper. We then go through each of the other five perspectives. After only 10–15 minutes, I know they understand what each perspective means and are ready to begin the activity for the first time. Neeld and Kiefer (1990) emphasize that the focus should be on moving students very quickly through each of the perspectives. However, elementary students need much more time. My purpose in using this writing strategy is to reinforce student learning on a mathematical concept, so I want to allow students adequate time to reflect and discuss what they know on a topic.

Depending on the grade and ability level, I may split the students up into six small groups, one per perspective. Then each group is assigned a specific perspective and handed a sheet of paper with the perspective written across the top. Each group brainstorms ideas for their perspective. After all of the groups are done writing their ideas, each group takes a turn sharing with the entire class the ideas generated. Other students listen and provide additional ideas and suggestions that the writers might want to incorporate into their perspective. After this sharing, each group writes a well-constructed paragraph based on the ideas brainstormed for their side.

Once the teacher is certain that students understand the strategy, the teacher may decide to have students work individually on the writing. Younger students might individually select one perspective and then construct a well-written paragraph on that topic. Older students and those needing an additional challenge may develop all six of the individual perspectives. Each perspective would then be incorporated into an individual paragraph that would be part of one well-written paper. Regardless of how this strategy is used, it takes time, but the process can be completed over several days.

One teacher decided to use this strategy with third-grade students. She chose the topic of telling time because the students frequently wanted to know why it was important to learn to tell time with analog clocks, since they felt that everyone could use digital clocks. Telling time was a topic the students had learned about, and they could explain it even if they had never thought about the topic from different perspectives.

First, the teacher had the entire class brainstorm ideas for each perspective on the topic. These ideas were each written by the teacher on chart paper. Since the students worked together as a class, their individual ideas helped the others think of additional contributions that might not have been articulated if the students had individually brainstormed the topic. Afterward, the students read through the entire list of ideas as the teacher read it orally to see if there were any additional thoughts they wanted to add. The entire process took approximately 10 minutes. The third graders came up with the following ideas for the sides:

1. Describe it: minutes, hours, seconds
2. Associate it: watches, alarm clocks, ovens, timers
3. Compare it: analog to digital
4. Analyze it: 60 seconds in a minute, 60 minutes in an hour

5. Apply it: getting to school on time, baking cookies, knowing when a television show comes on

6. Argue for or against it: to be on time, food doesn't get burned, Mom doesn't get mad

This list shows that the students knew a lot about telling time, and this brainstorming activity gave them an opportunity to relate a mathematical concept beyond the classroom walls to their everyday life. Many students use clocks and watches to let them know when a favorite television show is on and to get to school on time. Although the class could have argued for and against it, in this case the students only argued for telling time. They thought of many reasons why it was important to tell time, such as keeping their mothers happy. From the class discussion, it was evident that students were surprised at how much information they came up with on the topic. The results of this group brainstorming would be valuable for all students when it came time for the next part of the activity.

Once this prewriting activity was completed, the teacher had each student write on one perspective. They used the ideas brainstormed as a class as ideas for their paragraph. To make it more interesting, the teacher had each student roll a cube with one of the perspectives listed on each side to determine which perspective on telling time that student would write on. Each student completed a rough draft paragraph about time.

After rolling the cube, Cole's task was to apply telling time:

Clocks are Important

Because if there wern't clocks, we would be late for school, work, aso. And if we didn't have clocks we wouldn't know when our food is ready, and the house would catch, on fire and go Ka-boom!

Cole talked about two occasions when people apply time. First, he said that people need to use clocks so that they are not late for school. He also mentioned that clocks let people know when food is done cooking. Although some may feel that the students are arguing for telling time and the usage of clocks instead of merely applying the purpose of clocks, I often find that it is difficult for some young students to apply a topic without trying to argue for or against its use. When initially introducing each of the perspectives, teachers may determine that this is an excellent time to talk about the difference between persuasive writing and informative writing.

Another student, Anthony, described telling time. He immediately chose to write in great detail about a game system that is popular with many students, and therefore they can relate to what he wrote:

Discribe It

It tells time. It shows a hour hand, a minute hand, and a second hand. It also has a clock that shows the digital time. The digital time is digital, but military. (Which means there is such thing as 23:00.) It has numbers and hands on the clock face. The digital time (really military time) has only numbers.

It is obvious from his writing that Anthony has played the game a lot, and he writes in great detail about how the video game system shows time. In his description, he not only is extremely detailed but also uses a lot of terms related to telling time. He references the various hands on a clock, shows that he has knowledge of digital time, and even explains to the reader the concept of military time.

This third-grade class took a mathematical concept that they had learned in the past and examined it from a variety of perspectives. The students easily made connections to familiar experiences during classroom discussion and in their writing. After the activity, the teacher discussed each view, and many students orally shared their paragraphs. This is also an excellent time to reinforce that they successfully communicated their mathematical understanding with others.

Cubing takes more time than some of the other writing activities presented in this chapter because students have to think about a topic in a way that many have not done before. However, it is a great way to encourage students to take a more in-depth look at a mathematics concept. Students enjoy variety and strategies that provide a new twist on the common activity of writing. Cubing can provide a welcome change in many classrooms and help develop informative writing skills. Therefore, cubing is another writing strategy that teachers should keep in their repertoire of possible activities.

WHERE DO I GO FROM HERE?

By encouraging a wide variety of writing options with students, teachers can start the literacy–mathematics connection, maintain writing interest, and help students experience the many possibilities for communicating their mathematical knowledge. We must keep sight of our goals when teaching writing. While we work with students on the various activities suggested in this chapter, we must remember that our purpose is not to make sure that a specific piece of writing is written better but rather to make the students better writers (Anderson, 2000).

In this chapter, a variety of writing activities were shared. All of them have value and can tie together mathematics and writing. Determining which ones to use depends on the purpose for the writing and the needs of the students. The important thing to remember is that writing takes time, but it is time well spent with a worthwhile goal. Only by providing students with plenty of writing opportunities to communicate their mathematical knowledge are we allowing their abilities to develop. There are many other ways that teachers may choose to incorporate writing into the mathematics classroom. Hopefully this chapter provided the ideas necessary to get teachers thinking about possibilities to tie writing and mathematics together.

CHAPTER 4

Creating Powerful Poetry About Mathematical Concepts

first realized the power of poetry when I worked in urban schools as a reading consultant. During that time, I visited classrooms in an elementary school and taught poetry writing lessons to first- through fifth-grade classes. Students loved the lessons and talked about writing poetry with each other. One day as I walked down the hall, a student whose room I had not visited yet came up to me and said, "I can write poetry. Do you want to hear a poem I wrote?" He took a deep breath and then recited, "Roses are red. Violets are blue. I am a poet, and I love you." Then he stopped with a wide grin and waited for my reaction. Although there may have been some degree of plagiarism to his claim, I had to smile because he obviously felt proud to have modified and created a poem.

Although getting students to write can be a struggle, this one had already enthusiastically developed an idea without any prompting from me. However, one thing was also evident from the poem he shared: He held the common misconception that poetry should rhyme. Although students often feel that poetry must rhyme, there are many types of poetry that do not. Actually, when students aren't limited to using words that rhyme, it is often much easier for them to write poetry. In fact, Tompkins (2009) states that "rhyme is a sticking point for many would-be poets" (p. 371). When we help students create poetry, we must be ready to broaden their understanding of it and also recognize our purpose for asking them to write it.

Defining Poetry and Our Purpose

Poetry is a very difficult term to define. Even adults often disagree about what is and isn't poetry. In fact, Tompkins (2009) explains that the definition of poetry can be quite broad, and some forms may seem more like sentences than poems because there is a very fine dividing line between poetry and prose.

When I ask elementary students to explain poetry, their first reply often is that it rhymes, which could be due to the rhyming poems that children hear in the early years. Sometimes parents orally share Mother Goose rhymes with their children, and later on many students listen to teachers reading the famous and well-loved Shel Silverstein and Jack Prelutsky books. Although these are excellent books to get children interested in poetry, we need to move students beyond the idea that all poetry rhymes.

Within this chapter, a number of poetry trade books that can be easily integrated into the teaching of poetry are shared. Research supports the importance of exposing students to a variety of quality literature (Hansen, 2001; Lancia, 1997). Exposure to such texts not only provides a model of excellent writing for the students but it also gives students ideas for their own writing. By sharing a number of poetry books, we help students realize the wide variety of poetry that is available and allow them to broaden their definition of poetry.

This chapter also offers a variety of poetry experiences that educators might use with students in the classroom. Although none of the poetic forms discussed require rhyme, teachers may certainly choose to add rhyme as a poetic element. However, I would encourage educators to first introduce poetry writing that doesn't require rhyme. Students have difficulty thinking of words that rhyme and make sense in a poem, and it certainly limits the word-selection options. To make poetry writing easier for younger students and help them focus on the importance of meaning, it may be best to wait until students are older to encourage rhyme in poetry.

As shown through the examples discussed in this chapter, students can create poetry in the classroom to demonstrate their understanding of mathematical concepts. A variety of poetic forms are shared, and educators can select the ones that best meet their needs and goals. I have found that some of the best poetry is created by students as young as second grade. Poetry can be taught to even younger students, but based on my own experiences, it is often easier to create collaborative class poems in kindergarten and first grade.

Poetry and Mathematics: A Natural Connection

In the early elementary grades, many students are developing their affective skills. At this stage, they determine whether mathematics is interesting and something at which they can be successful. The opinions and attitudes developed when students are young will influence the future success they have with mathematics. We must provide students with positive experiences that they enjoy and through which can achieve success. Integrating poetry and mathematics through developmentally appropriate experiences can do just that. We not only foster a love and interest in both mathematics and literacy but also help students make connections between the two content areas.

Creating poetry is also an activity that lends itself well to group work. Therefore, many of the ideas discussed in this chapter can easily be used with heterogeneous groups. NCTM (2000) strongly encourages teachers to allow students to work in groups and foster the creation of mathematical communities. The importance of group work is also reflected in the literacy community, and literacy research shows that students can learn from one another when working in groups (Eeds & Wells, 1991). Through collaboration and dialogue, students scaffold each other's learning through their social interaction (Vygotsky, 1962).

By working in a group to create a poem, students listen to, think about, and discuss mathematical concepts. The discussion supported in heterogeneous groups helps struggling learners talk about mathematical concepts more easily. In small groups, students feel free to take risks and refine their understanding of mathematical content. Plus, as a benefit to the teacher, a great deal of information can be gained just by listening to students when they work with others. In fact, researchers found that as students share and discuss mathematical ideas, teachers can discover misconceptions that students may have about the content material (Tanner & Casados, 1998).

Helping students adjust their written language, use different writing processes, and create texts representative of a variety of genre are all goals of the English language arts standards (IRA & NCTE, 1996). Standards 4–6 (see Appendix A) discuss the need for students to be able to create print for a variety of purposes. Furthermore, the NCTM (2000) Communication Standard (see Appendix B) supports the importance of having all students in kindergarten through 12th grade share and express their mathematical knowledge in a well-written manner. All of these standards can be demonstrated through the poetry experiences discussed in this chapter.

Starting With a Formula

The first four types of poetry discussed are known as formula poems. These are very easy to write at even the youngest grades, so I often find that this type of poetry is a good starting place for students. The simplistic nature of the poems makes it possible for all students to achieve success. Once students know the pattern for the formula poem, they will be able to create their own excellent examples. Also, formula poems allow students to focus more on the thoughts they want to express rather than the elements of poetry (Cecil, 1994).

"...Is" Poems

In this type of formula poetry, each line in the poem explains or defines the topic discussed. The teacher may decide to have a broad topic like mathematics for the focus of the poem. If that is the case, then each line will begin with "Mathematics is...." This is an excellent opportunity for students to relate mathematics to the world around them. What is mathematics? How is it used in the world? Although time is often limited with all of the other instructional considerations teachers must make, even those educators with very little time can share a quick example of mathematical writing through this type of poetry.

To help students think about the meaning of mathematics and the manner in which it relates to the world, I like to share two of my favorite poems from *Marvelous Math: A Book of Poems* (Hopkins, 2001). Students at all grade levels love hearing and discussing the poems in this book. I have never had any difficulty getting students excited about poetry, and research has shown that children at a very young age like listening to it (Fisher & Natarella, 1982; Kutiper & Wilson, 1993).

One of my favorite poems in the collection is O'Neill's (Hopkins, 2001) example from "Take a Number." You might begin by asking students if they would like to live in a world without mathematics. How would their days and years be different? Do they think it would be enjoyable to not worry about mathematics? After a brief discussion, share O'Neill's poem with them. Through the words in the poem, students can easily envision a world where mathematics doesn't exist. Even students who may not love math can't help but realize its importance in their lives after hearing and discussing the poem.

> Imagine a world
> Without mathematics:
> No rulers or scales,
> No inches or feet,
> No dates or numbers
> On house or street,
> No prices or weights,
> No determining heights,
> No hours running through
> Days and nights.
> No zero, no birthdays,
> No way to subtract
> All of the guesswork
> Surrounding the fact.
> No sizes for shoes,
> Or suit or hat....
> Wouldn't it be awful to live like that?

From TAKE A NUMBER by Mary O'Neill. Copyright © 1968 by Mary O'Neill. © renewed 1996 by Erin Baroni and Abigail Hagier. Used by permission of Marian Reiner.

This poem shares with students how different the world would be without mathematics. The poem helps them begin thinking about mathematics and the necessity of it in their daily lives. Many familiar concepts like street numbers, birthdays, and clothing sizes are taken for granted. After sharing the poem, students can brainstorm other ideas for how their lives would be different without mathematics. How would they call their friends without telephone numbers? If there were no clocks, how would they know when to go to school or when to arrive at a best friend's party? What would happen if people didn't know how fast their automobile traveled on the road? Would it still be fun to play games if there were no way to keep score? These are just some of the things that students could think and talk about in their discussion.

A second poem I share from the same collection helps students realize how comforting and predictable math can be. Franco's (Hopkins, 2001)

"Math Makes Me Feel Safe" reinforces the idea that quality poetry doesn't have to rhyme. By sharing examples like this, students expand their view of what constitutes poetry:

> Math isn't just adding
> and subtracting.
> Not for me.
> Math makes me feel safe
> knowing that my brother will always be
> three years younger than I am,
> and every day of the year will have
> twenty-four hours.
> That a snowflake landing on my mitten
> will have exactly six points,
> and that I can make new shapes
> from my Tangram pieces
> whenever I feel lonely.
> Math isn't just adding
> and subtracting,
> Not for me.
> Math makes me feel safe.

From Franco, B. (2001). Math makes me feel safe. In L.B. Hopkins (Ed.), *Marvelous math: A book of poems*. New York: Alladin. Reprinted with permission.

After listening to this poem, students can discuss what math means to them. What aspects of math are comfortably predictable in their life? Perhaps they enjoy knowing that some of their favorite holidays are on the same day every year. They might enjoy knowing there are always four quarters in a football game, or perhaps they appreciate the fact that they can always count on watching their favorite television show at a certain time on a specific television channel.

Sharing poems like these is important. It provides an opportunity for students to see adults modeling fluent reading during a read-aloud. Also, it allows students an opportunity to get hooked on books and a genre they might not have considered reading. Finally, it helps students see how authors communicate their mathematical knowledge through poetry and reinforces the importance of tying writing and mathematics together. Through listening or reading children's literature, students realize that authors value communicating mathematical knowledge, and students are exposed to quality writing.

Students in a first-grade elementary classroom were encouraged to think about what mathematics meant to them. Then the teacher explained that they would be creating "...is" poems. As a group, the students would write a definition for math, and every line would begin with "Math is." As the class listened and watched, the teacher wrote, "Math is _____." on the board, then she encouraged students to give ideas that might complete the sentence. Even though the students were young, they did an amazing job. The following collaborative poem was created:

Math is adding and subtracting.
Math is adding a boy and a girl together to make a family.
Math is adding three and three is six.
Math is a calendar.
Math is at the store.

The students immediately thought about their recent mathematical learning. They were able to relate adding and subtracting to more than just numerals. The teacher asked the students to clarify any answers that were unclear. When a little boy replied, "Math is a calendar," she asked him to explain what he meant by that comment. He immediately made a text connection and talked about how they had a calendar in their math book. Since several students wanted to volunteer "Math is at the store," they elaborated where they saw math at the store. Some referred to using money to buy items they wanted, and others stated that math books could be bought at the store to practice skills at home.

When creating a class poem, teachers and students can both gain from the experience. The teacher can learn a lot through the oral discussion about what previous knowledge the students have on the topic of mathematics, and ideas that are provided orally help students better understand mathematics. Although creating a class poem is a great activity, and students will enjoy rereading the poem that they created at a later time, the process is as important as the product. Teachers may have students write on a broad topic like mathematics or on a much narrower concept, such as a specific shape, a type of angle, an operation such as subtraction or multiplication, odd numbers, or specific numbers. This is an excellent way to incorporate a current mathematical concept that the students are learning in school and a way to assess their knowledge of that concept.

One group of fifth-grade students was introduced to the idea of ...is poems, and the teacher shared that the poems can be written about a variety of mathematical concepts. The students orally brainstormed possible topics, such as perimeter, tessellations, and angles, that they might choose from for their individual poems. Then students each selected a topic from the ideas shared and wrote their own ...is poems about math.

Algernique, a fifth grader, wrote an ...is poem to explain her thinking about mathematics:

Angles are the squares on the carpet.
Angles are the tiles on the cieling.
Angles are acute on pieces of cake.
Angels are right angles when I put my glasses on.
Angels are my legs when I bend them.

In her poem, Algernique does an excellent job of defining angles by relating the subject to her personal life. She relates mathematics to experiences both inside the classroom context and outside the school. Algernique looked around the classroom and noticed the squares on the carpet that were made of two angles, and she looked at the tiles on the ceiling. She considered other ways that she could show an angle. Algernique mentioned that when she puts her eyeglasses on, the frame makes a right angle, and her legs form an angle when she bends them. She thought about ideas outside of the school where she might see angles and mentioned the acute angles that are seen when a cake is sliced. In her poem, Algernique demonstrates that she can communicate her mathematical knowledge and connect it to the outside world, and she shows that she understands the importance of mathematics.

With this type of formula poetry, I often need to emphasize that length is not the most important quality when writing the poems. Many students want to write as many lines as they can about a topic, believing that more is definitely better. If I find that students are writing an excessive amount of lines just to add length and are not really thinking about the content, I encourage them to reflect on the lines they have written and select the 5 or 10 best lines for their final draft. The length expected depends greatly on the ages and abilities of the students involved. The teacher may even create a class poem or allow the students to work in pairs. Students need to think about the topic, communicate their ideas to the best of their abilities, and develop an understanding of how literacy and mathematics can be tied together in an activity in which they are able to achieve success.

ABC Poems

ABC poems are another type of formula poem that is relatively easy for students to write. In this type of poetry, each line begins with a consecutive letter of the alphabet. The first decision is choosing which letter will begin the poem. A teacher may have all of the students start the first line of their poems with the same letter or the letter A. However, another option that tends to make the activity a little more interesting for the students is for the teacher to put each of the letters of the alphabet on individual note cards, place those cards in a bag, and allow each child to select a card from the bag. The letter chosen will begin the first line of that student's poem.

Two teachers decided to use this type of poetry near the end of the school year as a fun way to review the students' mathematical learning over the year. As can be seen in the following poem, one second grader, Lindsey, began her poem with the letter *M* and continued through the letter *V* to create a 10-line poem:

Math
M ultiplication is the opposite of division.
N ovember is the 11th month.
O ctober is one of the months that have 31 days.
P erimeter is around a shape.
Q urters are made silver and worth 25 cents.
R ectangles are a prism.
S quare pattern blocks are orange.
T riangles have 3 sides.
U is in the month of June and July, the sixth and seventh months.
V ertex is where Lines come together.

Lindsey's poem reveals that she understands a lot about mathematics, and there are a number of concepts with which she is familiar, such as perimeter, monetary units, vertex, and prisms. This poem enables the teacher to see which concepts Lindsey can articulate and helps Lindsey realize just how much she has learned in mathematics. By orally sharing the poetry and discussing the mathematical concepts mentioned in the poems, even greater learning can occur.

A fourth grader also created an ABC poem. However, the student expanded upon the basic idea of ABC poetry. Although the poem is shorter than some of the others written, it contains many poetic elements and shares a great deal of information:

> Cubic measure. Cubic foot, Cubic inch, Cubic yard. Why so many measurements.
> Division, the hard kind. Full of long, tedious steps. Why must there be a
>   remainder.
> Estimate. No thanks! It's not the real answer. Why is that ok?
> Fractions. Equal, Mixed, improper fractions. Decimals are the hardest!
> Graphs. Line, Bar, Pie, and picture. Many different shapes, ways, and colors.

This student not only demonstrates an understanding of various mathematical concepts but also uses poetic elements like repetition, phrasing, and line extension to communicate ideas. The ABC poem from C to G demonstrates an understanding of estimating, the awareness that similar information can be shared through a variety of graphs, and knowledge that the term *cubic* can be used to describe a number of measurements. Furthermore, the poem shows which mathematical concepts the student finds more difficult than others.

"I Used to Think…, but Now I Know" Poems

While writing poetry has been shown to easily integrate into mathematics (Altieri, 2005, 2009), the formula poem called "I used to think…, but now I know" is especially beneficial because students can demonstrate metacognitive awareness and show growth in how their mathematical thinking changes over time.

Often the easiest way to get started with this type of poetry is to have the students reflect back on how they have changed since they were little. Although that may seem a little more difficult to do with very young students, we have all heard even the youngest ones refer to when they were small or younger. If teachers wish to share some examples of this form of poetry, they may want to read some poems from Koch's (1970) *Wishes, Lies, and Dreams: Teaching Children to Write Poetry*. Then the students can discuss how they are different from their younger siblings or cousins.

When working with very young students, the teacher may share a book such as *When I Was Little: A Four-Year-Old's Memoir of Her Youth* (Curtis, 1995). I have found this book to be well received by kindergarteners and first graders. This text can easily lead students into a discussion about their own "youth." For instance, I explained to some third graders that I wanted them to think about how they had changed since they were little. I explained the type of poem they would be writing that day and told them that the lines would be written in pairs. Each pair of lines would begin as follows:

I used to _____,
But now I _____.

Immediately the students had many ideas to share. They wanted to talk about how their life as a baby compared with their life now. A few mentioned drinking from a bottle, but some had trouble remembering that long ago because they would only know of their life as infants from secondhand information shared by others or through photos they had seen of themselves. To expand their ideas, we discussed that they did not need to remember all the way back to when they were a baby. They might think about when they were younger and just starting school. They changed in so many ways over the years since kindergarten.

One little boy said, "I used to laugh all the time." I asked what was different now, and he said, "But now I don't." We talked about how they can write the poem and select words so that the meaning is even clearer for the reader. One student said he cried a lot when he was younger. I encouraged him to think about what he did now instead of crying, and he replied, "talk." By working through a few possible lines with the students, the poetic form was explained easily.

Students can then think about their mathematical knowledge and how it has changed. What is a math concept that they have learned? What is an opinion about mathematics that has changed over the years? Is there a mathematical misconception that was explained? How is their mathematical thinking different now from the beginning of the year?

Whether a teacher decides to have students write a general poem about how they have changed before proceeding to a poem about how their mathematical thinking has changed depends upon the students and teacher. Like any type of poetry, a lot of flexibility exists, and there is no one right way to teach the form.

One teacher incorporated "I used to think…, but now I know" poetry into her classroom, and Tiesha, a second grader, wrote the following:

I used to multiply but now I divide.
I used to read digital clocks but now I read analog.
I used to count by 2's but now I count by ten's.
I used to measure in inches but now I measure in centimeters.
I used to guess but now I estimate.

It is amazing what can be learned about a student's mathematical growth with only five lines. In her poem, Tiesha uses a number of mathematical terms and discusses many new words that she has learned during the past school year, including analog, estimate, and metric terms. This vocabulary development in itself is important because research has shown that developing vocabulary is integral to students' success in school (Becker, 1977; McKeown, Beck, Omanson, & Perfetti, 1983). In fact, a limited vocabulary has been shown to play a key role in the failure of at-risk students (White, Graves, & Slater, 1990). Therefore, as educators, we need to do all we can to help students develop their vocabulary in key areas like mathematics. By writing mathematical terms in a poem and later rereading the poem, students reinforce the concepts, and the words gradually become second nature.

The poems not only provide information for both the teacher and the students but also document the students' learning. Often teachers keep portfolios or folders of student work to demonstrate growth, and including a variety of poetry artifacts can only strengthen the collection. By having students create this type of poetry at various points during the year, they can reflect on the new learning that has occurred and show growth in mathematical knowledge and literacy skills.

"I Don't Understand" Poems

Although this form of poetry is as easy to write as the previous types discussed, often these formula poems allow the teacher to see the struggles that students are dealing with as they learn mathematical concepts andto determine which concepts may need further explanation. "I don't understand" poetry can be written in a manner similar to "I used to think..., but now I know" poems, with alternate line patterns. When using this formula, alternating lines of the poem are "I don't understand _____" and "But I do understand _____." However, teachers may also choose to change the style of the last line. In that case, all of the lines would begin with "I don't understand" except for the last line of the poem, which would begin "But I do understand."

In one third-grade class, the teacher asked students to think about what they had learned in math that year. She wanted the students to talk about any mathematical concepts that were really tough for them to understand. Were there any terms that they struggled with in class? The students then wrote individual poems. Melvin shared his confusion in his poem:

I Don't understand why I have to devide.
I don't understand why you have to start with the highest number when you
    devide.
I don't understand why we have to do times.
But I do understand addition and subtracting.

When students complete this type of formula poem individually, they are often apt to share with the teacher problems they might not share in front of their peers. Melvin makes it clear in his poem that he is struggling with understanding division. He isn't even sure why they start with the highest number when dividing. However, he also seems frustrated because he doesn't understand the relevance of some of the material that he is learning. Melvin questions why they are even learning to multiply and divide.

After reading Melvin's poem and the poems of his classmates, the teacher may want to reinforce certain concepts, perhaps by relating the mathematical concepts to their lives outside of school. Teachers can have special activities for small groups of students who are struggling with the same mathematical concepts or have those students work with others who have a deeper understanding of that concept. This type of poetry can provide a lot of information to the teacher.

The types of formula poems discussed in this chapter provide an excellent opportunity for students of any age to organize their mathematical thoughts and convey these ideas to others. Students are constantly developing dispositions toward math, and we want these to be positive. Creating a formula poem is a simple way for all students to achieve success in both literacy and mathematics. Allowing students to reflect on their increased understanding of mathematics can only strengthen positive attitudes toward the content area.

Creating Poetic Puzzles

Students love puzzles and games, and often they associate those activities with play more than school. Riddles are one type of puzzle, and students tend to view riddles as fun activities and therefore forget that they are learning in the process. In fact, I find riddles to be the perfect type of puzzles for students of all ages. Through sharing, students develop higher level thinking skills as they listen to the riddles, narrow down the possible answers, and make conclusions based on the clues given (Buchoff, 1996). Not only are there a variety of children's books available to share with diverse grades but also riddles can easily be tied into the mathematics curriculum.

When I first started sharing riddles with elementary students as a reading consultant, I was amazed at how much the students loved them. They saw riddles as puzzles and wanted to be successful in solving them. It struck me as funny that I would visit a classroom with a book of riddles, and days or even weeks later I would see the same students in the hallway where they would ask me if I could bring the same picture book of riddles back to their classroom. I explained that they already knew the answers from when we figured out the riddles together prior, but they didn't care. Thus, I decided to build on this interest and enthusiasm for riddles so students could develop their reasoning skills and understand how to solve riddles through practice.

By doing this, I realized how difficult riddles can be for students to solve due to the thought processes involved in determining the answer. Students really have to think about all of the clues. I often talked students through the lines of poems in the picture book *Riddle-icious* (Lewis, 1996) because students would not take into consideration all of the clues in the riddles when shouting out an answer. The pictures in that book give away the answer. However, when the students listen to the riddles without viewing the pages, the riddles present a challenge for many students in elementary school. Sharing riddles with students and then helping them work through the thought processes necessary to understand the solution is important.

Before students can create their own riddles, they must understand the type of thinking that riddles demand. There are a number of well-written mathematical riddle books available to share with students. Often students enjoy books like *Arithme-tickle: An Even Number of Odd Riddle-Rhymes* (Lewis, 2002) and *Math for All Seasons* (Tang, 2002). Tang has written a number of mathematical riddle books designed for all ages from preschool through middle school.

Once students start to enjoy solving riddles, they can easily move on to writing them. After solving the riddles in books as a class, I decided to have students write their own. They were very enthusiastic. The first step was to look at riddles and help establish some guidelines for writing them. Obviously riddles shouldn't be too easy to solve because then they don't provide a challenge for the reader, but I had to reinforce that the students didn't want their riddles to be so difficult that no one could solve them. At the same time, the clues provided in a riddle needed to progressively reveal the answer. If the clue in the first line reveals the answer, then there is no reason for anyone to read the rest of the riddle.

The simplicity of the riddles depends on the ages and ability levels of the students. When I worked with classes on writing riddles, I gave each student a topic for their riddle on a small folded piece of paper. Along with the teacher's assistance, I provided appropriate terms to all of the students. If the student was an EL and just developing a basic vocabulary, I selected a more common term that the teacher felt the student would know. The students took great care to sneak a look at their topic and then carefully cover the term written on their paper so their classmates wouldn't see the word. That way the riddle would truly be a puzzle. The students quickly figured out how to write riddles and asked to use vocabulary from content areas as topics. This strategy is an excellent way to reinforce writing and mathematics.

For very young students and those whose literacy skills are just emerging, I initially focus on having students write three to five clues (depending on age and ability) about a mathematical concept. It may be easiest to create the first riddle together as a class. If students have difficulty coming up with a topic, allow them to choose one from a list of mathematical concepts brainstormed by the class.

One first-grade teacher found an excellent way to incorporate math riddles in her classroom of 6- and 7-year-olds. Since the beginning of the school year, her class had been working on number recognition and counting to 100. They had shared a number of books, including *From One to One Hundred* (Sloat, 1995) and *One Hundred Hungry Ants* (Pinczes, 1999). Recently the students had started working on place value and counting to 100 by twos, fives, and so on.

Because writing riddles was a new idea for both the teacher and the students, the teacher initially decided to work with a small group of students. She pulled a group of high-achieving students aside, and together they looked at a chart with numbers listed from one to 100. Then the students selected a number from the chart and created clues to reveal which number they were describing. Similar to my own experiences, the teacher had to remind several of the students to be sure they were gradually narrowing down the clues.

After the students created their riddles, they shared them with the rest of the class. The class was so excited about solving the riddles that the other students wanted to learn to write them, too. One student created the following riddle:

> You do not cawnt me when you cawnt by twos.
> I have two digits.
> My last digit is nine.
> When you add my two numbers the sum is eighteen.
> What number am I?

Very young students, such as the ones in this first-grade class, can enjoy writing riddles, but the task can also be modified to challenge older students, who can also incorporate a number of poetic concepts into the riddles they create.

One fourth-grade teacher decided to incorporate writing riddles into her curriculum and shared some excellent children's literature to introduce riddles. She chose to begin a math lesson with several examples from *ABC Math Riddles* (Martin, 2003) and *Shape Up!* (Adler, 2000). The following poem from *ABC Math Riddles* was shared on the white board in her classroom:

> My name begins with L,
> there's an E at the end.
> I'm a set of points,
> and I will never bend.
> Some think I curve.
> Some think I swerve.
> But I am always straight.
> What am I? Please state!

From Martin, J. (2003). *ABC math riddles.* Columbus, NC: Peel Productions. Reprinted with permission.

After sharing and discussing some of the riddles in these books, the teacher then explained to her students that they would create a riddle using geometry as the subject. The students were instructed to include elements of rhythm and rhyme in their riddles as well as a question. Since the students had already completed a rather comprehensive unit on poetry, the teacher knew the students were aware of the different elements of poetry, so she encouraged them to include elements such as alliteration, onomatopoeia, repetition, and imagery. Furthermore, the students were informed that they must include factual information about the geometric concept or object that they chose. Finally, the entire class brainstormed possible topics that the students could use for their riddles. Kelly created the following riddle for her classmates:

> My name begins with P.
> And the middle is L.
> My lines never cross.
> Or intersect as well.
> I never curve, swerve, or bend.
> I don't have sides just lines.
> Can you guess what I am?
> I hope you can.

Kelly modeled her writing after the example the teacher shared. Kelly gave clues to the spelling of the word by telling the reader that the initial letter of the mathematical concept is a *P* and that an *L* is found near the middle of the word. She also included traits of the geometric concept. The reader knows after reading the riddle that the concept involves lines that do not cross, intersect, or bend. Finally, the reader of the poem knows that the mathematical concept has lines but no sides. Through all of these clues, the reader is able to narrow the possible answer to parallel lines.

Blake, another fourth-grade student in the class, chose to create a riddle about a shape. Similar to Kelly's riddle, Blake chose to give clues to the word and also traits of the shape. In addition, he included clues about where this mathematical concept might be seen outside the classroom and what sort of reaction this shape elicits. Blake's riddle about an octagon revealed that he understands the context in which a person might see the shape (i.e., a stop sign) and traits of the shape (i.e., all lines, no rays, eight sides):

Who Am I?
I start with a letter next to N in the alphabet,
But that's not enough you don't know me yet!
I tell you to stop so you better obey.
Me, all lines and never a ray.
My sides are between 9 and 7,
Still don't know me, well it's not 11.
Sometimes I'm next to the street,
But you wouldn't walk on me, not with your feet!
Now you should know me, do you, or not?
Who am I? Give it a thought.
STOP!

Riddles are fun for all ages and have been popular for decades. There is something addictive about riddles, and many students can't seem to get enough of them. Riddles can often be difficult to understand for very young student, because they require a way of thinking that is more abstract. However, with a little guidance even young learners can appreciate and enjoy them. By allowing students to write riddles, teachers can help demystify them. Solving riddles is like many skills in that the only way to improve is through practice. Once students understand the type of thinking involved and the way riddles are set up, they can be successful riddle writers and solvers. Using an engaging activity like riddles to connect literacy and mathematics is a great teaching tool. Writing mathematical riddles will help students develop the higher level of thought necessary to solve them and provide an enjoyable way for students to demonstrate their mathematical knowledge.

Providing More Challenging Poetry-Writing Activities

Although slightly more challenging, both preposition poems and poems for multiple voices have a place in the classroom and provide a great deal of educational value for the students and the teacher. Preposition poems reinforce the concept of prepositional phrases while helping students relate mathematics to the world around them. Poems for multiple voices require students to develop fluency and phrasing so that the different voices reading the lines make sense. Similar to other types of poetry previously discussed in this chapter, these two types of poetry can help students reinforce and expand their thinking about math as they make the literacy–mathematics connection.

Preposition Poems

This type of poetry is more difficult than some of the previously mentioned forms because students must already understand prepositional phrases to write the poems. Tompkins (2009) suggests that teachers provide students with a list of prepositional phrases, which can be helpful. I have seen some amazing poems created by rather young children. Often teachers begin this type of poetry experience by reviewing the information that students know about prepositional phrases. Sometimes teachers choose to share a picture book with students, such as Heller's (1998) *Behind the Mask: A Book About Prepositions* or Cleary's (2003) *Under, Over, by the Clover: What Is a Preposition?* After reading and discussing the book, teachers may use a teacher-created list of prepositional phrases or let the class brainstorm a list.

After reviewing a list of prepositional phrases with her class, one fourth-grade teacher then established the following guidelines for creating a preposition poem:

- Each line must start with a preposition (you may choose which ones to use).
- Your poem must be geometry related (you may choose a specific shape, angle, etc.).
- Each poem should be at least six lines long.

Then the teacher provided the class with the following example of a preposition poem she created about acute angles to help guide their work:

Acute Angles
On the tops of houses
Inside of the bike's wheel
Along the hands of the clock

This teacher-created example is excellent because it mentions places with which students might not automatically associate when they think about the term *acute angle*, and yet all three examples in the poem are items with which they are familiar. Also, the poem doesn't rhyme, which helps students realize that they can write quality poetry without limiting their word choice to words with specific endings.

After reading the example as a class, students were then allowed time in small groups to write their own poems while the teacher monitored the group work. Three of the students created a preposition poem about parallel lines:

Parallel Lines

Along the edges of the paper
Beneath the covers of a book
Across the top of the podium
Around the perimeter of the board
Within the edges of a window
Below the seat of the stool
Through the tunnels of the tracks.

The poem shows not only that the students grasped the concept of parallel lines but also that they can apply the mathematical concept to real-life situations. The podium, piece of paper, book, board, and window mentioned in the poem were all objects that they could see in the environment while they were writing. Likewise, three other students chose to write a preposition poem about perpendicular lines:

Perpendicular Lines

Along the path in the woods.
On the lines of the big, red, crate
Toward the middle of the calendar
Within the long and tall book shelf
Through the letter "T."
Above a church is a big cross.

Preposition poems help students reinforce their knowledge about prepositions while allowing them to demonstrate their understanding of a variety of mathematical concepts. Although this is often considered a difficult form of poetry, the task will be easier for students working in groups. Students benefit from the discussion they have within their group and develop their oral language skills through collaboration. Finally, this type of poetry encourages students to relate the concepts to the world around them.

Poems for Multiple Voices

These poems are written in side-by-side columns, and each column is read by a different individual or group of readers (Tompkins, 2009). While Tompkins refers to these poems as *poems for two voices*, I prefer the term *multiple voices* because these poems can involve numerous voices reading the lines aloud. Although many educators have shared poems that were written to be read by more than one person, I have found that very few teachers have actually tried *writing* this type of poetry with the students in their classroom. I think this is due in large part to the complexity of completing such a task. It wasn't until I worked with a graduate class composed of practicing teachers who attempted to create this type of poetry in their classrooms that I realized the difficulties. After several of the teachers came back to class and informed me that it wasn't working, I realized that I needed to explicitly model how these poems could be created.

After discussing some specific suggestions, which are shared in this section, the teachers were able to help their students successfully create this type of poetry. I believe that poems for multiple voices are still one of the more difficult types of poetry to write, so teachers may choose to have their students write different forms of poetry initially or perhaps use this type to provide an additional challenge for some students.

Teachers may want to consider introducing this type of poetry to their students with a trade book containing examples of poems for multiple voices. One book that upper elementary teachers may wish to share with their students is Fleischman's (2008) *Big Talk: Poems for Four Voices*. Although teachers may have heard of poems for two voices, Fleischman created this book so that four different people or groups can read each poem. At the beginning of the book, the author provides hints for helping students understand how to read the poems. Each line is highlighted in green, yellow, orange, or purple, which makes it easy for students to know when it is their turn to read. Some of the poems are more difficult to read, but the author arranged them so that the book starts with the easiest examples and progresses to the more difficult.

Another possible book to show students is a text specifically containing mathematical poems for multiple voices. Although most of the poems in *Math Talk: Mathematical Ideas in Poems for Two Voices* (Pappas, 1993) are too difficult for elementary students due to the mathematical content, several of them contain appropriate grade-level material. Upper elementary students may enjoy the poems about squares and triangles. Many of the poems in the book describe one mathematical concept; however, I have found that it is easier to use poems for multiple voices to compare and contrast a topic.

Although poetry for multiple voices is often seen as a challenging type of poetry, one teacher decided to introduce it to a class of kindergarteners. The students were learning about money, so the teacher had the class create a poem about the penny and the dollar. She began by reading the book *Jenny Found a Penny* (Harris, 2008). As the teacher read the book aloud, the students were eager to talk about saving money and share the knowledge they had about pennies and other coins.

After the discussion, the teacher held up a dollar bill and a penny. She told the students they would share everything they knew about the dollar and the penny to create a class poem. Then she said that they were going to talk about how the dollar and penny were similar. The students volunteered the following ideas, which the teacher listed on a wall chart:

> They are both money.
> They both have presidents on them.
> You save them in your piggy bank.
> You can buy things with them.

She made the activity into an interactive writing activity. After the list was complete, the teacher read the list orally to the class, and then they chorally read the list as she moved her hand from left to right underneath the sentences.

Then she stated that they were going to talk about ways in which the dollar and penny were different. She encouraged the students to think about the appearance of the dollar and the penny to decide which they would rather have and why. The students came up with the following lists of ideas for each, and as the teacher repeated their ideas out loud, the teacher and students wrote them on the board:

Dollar	Penny
100 cents	1 cent
George Washington	Abraham Lincoln
More	Less

The teacher then took the two lists and created a class poem for the students, which was then written on a wall chart:

Money

Dollar

Penny

100 cents

1 cent

They both are money.

George Washington

Abraham Lincoln

They both have presidents on them.

More

Less

You save them in your piggy bank.
You can buy things with them.
Money

Because this was a very young group of students, the teacher explained that poems are sometimes written and read differently than the type of text they normally see. The teacher shared with them Hoberman's (2001) book *You Read to Me, I'll Read to You: Very Short Stories to Read Together*, which uses color-coded text to help even the youngest readers understand poems for multiple voices. Teachers who enjoy using this book may want to review *You Read to Me, I'll Read to You: Very Short Scary Tales to Read Together* (Hoberman, 2007). Also, students may enjoy seeing some familiar fairy tale characters in *You Read to Me, I'll Read to You: Very Short Fairy Tales to Read Together* (Hoberman, 2004). These three books are an excellent way to introduce a unique type of poetry to even the youngest of children.

After sharing the book, the teacher told the students that the poem they created as a class about money is similar to the examples in the book. The students would read from left to right and top to bottom, but sometimes one person might read one line and another person might read a different line. She reminded them that this type of poem was written differently than a lot of text that they had previously read in class.

When reading a poem like this aloud with young students, the teacher may want to model how it will sound with another teacher or a paraprofessional. The teacher can record the oral reading of the poem, then play the recording for the students, as they follow along with the wall chart. When it is time for the students to read the poem, the class can be physically divided into two groups. The teacher might choose to read the center column while the groups each have either the right or left column to read.

Creating a poem for multiple voices was a valuable activity for this teacher and her students as it provided the students with a chance to review the concept of money, which they were currently learning in class. The activity also introduced the students to a new type of poetry, thus their schema for poetry was expanded. Also, the students were proud of their class creation and loved to hear how it sounded and know that they wrote the poem.

In another classroom, third graders were introduced to poems for multiple voices. Although the topic of the poem was measurement, creating the poem required the students to discriminate between measuring large and small amounts of liquids and measuring distances. The teacher began by explaining that the class would write a poem about the topic of measurement. She wrote the concept, measurement, at the top of a wall chart, then underneath she wrote the word *measuring* over two columns. The third-grade students were asked to list some liquid measurements they use or have seen used at home. As the class talked, she wrote the types of measurement that might be used to measure small amounts in the left-hand column and the ones that would be used to measure larger amounts in the right-hand column. Then as a class, they discussed when they might use the specific types of measurement. When using teaspoons, tablespoons, and cups, the students immediately thought about baking cookies. They also said that pints, quarts, and gallons were used to make sweet tea. By the time this discussion was completed, the class had written the first half of the poem:

Measurement

Measuring Liquids

Tablespoon, teaspoon, cups	
	Pints, quarts, gallons
We measure liquids to bake cookies.	We measure liquids to
	make sweet tea.

Then the teacher proceeded to help the class complete the second half of the poem in the same manner. They discussed measuring something short and also measuring a long distance. This classroom talk involved sharing the units of measurement used and also knowing when they might want to use that type of measurement. After that, the teacher added the last three lines to complete the poem. The class talked about how two groups would read the poem. If the same words were in both columns on the same line, then the line would be read at the same time, thus sometimes all of the students would read the same line, and sometimes only one group would read. The teacher would read the center column. The class divided into two groups to read the completed poem:

Measurement

Measuring Liquids

Tablespoon, teaspoon, cups

Pints, quarts, gallons

We measure liquids to   We measure liquids to
bake cookies.

make sweet tea.

Measuring Distance

Inches, Feet, Yards

Miles

We measure distance to   We measure distance to
see how   see how
much we've grown.

far we've traveled.

Measurement
You use it EVERY day!
Measurement

Teachers may want to underline the lines that vary from one column to another column in order to draw students' attention to those lines. Another idea is to color-code lines and assign a different color to each group, so the students remember what lines they are to read. The poems about money and measurement can serve as excellent examples of poems for multiple voices. This type of poetry can be written to compare and contrast a number of mathematical concepts. The following is a list of other possible topics:

- Analog clocks versus digital clocks
- American customary system versus the metric system
- Guessing versus estimating

- Acute angles versus obtuse angles

- Word problems versus equations

- Subtraction versus addition

- Comparison of shapes

- Representation, such as pie graphs versus charts

- Even numbers versus odd numbers

Benefits of the Poetry Experience

The benefits of students developing language skills through reading poetry (Hadaway, Vardell, & Young, 2001) and writing poetry (Kiefer et al., 2006) have been well documented. After writing, students should be given the opportunity to share and read aloud their poems. According to Routman (2000), students often don't consider themselves poets until they read poems written by children. Therefore, it is important for students to create poetry to share with their peers.

Younger students enjoy chorally reading lines of poetry as a class or in groups. By chorally reading the lines, they develop their sight word knowledge, improve fluency with rereading, and reinforce their mathematical knowledge. The scaffolding provided by hearing peers read the poetry and the repetition found in formula poetry can be especially beneficial for ELs and struggling readers and writers.

Poetry can be enjoyed again and again. Students may select some of the poems they created and record them. Later these recordings can be used in listening centers or sent home for the students to share with their parents. Another suggestion is to display the student-created poetry on the walls around the room, read the poems on the morning announcements, share some of the poems in a weekly classroom newspaper to show parents what students are learning, or present the poems as part of a literacy celebration for other classrooms or parents to enjoy.

WHERE DO I GO FROM HERE?

Students are not the only ones who reap the benefits of writing poetry. Educators also benefit from creating a classroom of poets. Through reading and discussing student-created poetry, it is possible to assess what students know about various mathematical concepts. This type of informal assessment takes much less time than formal tests, can be done more frequently, and provides important information to help guide the teacher's instruction. The information gleaned from the mathematical poems can affect future literacy and mathematical instruction. Teachers may use the information to clear up mathematical misunderstandings and strengthen areas in which the students already have a firm knowledge. By examining what students write about mathematical concepts, teachers are better able to provide appropriate instruction for all students in their classrooms.

Strengthening student connections between mathematics and literacy is vital. By allowing students to create mathematical poetry, we help them deepen their mathematical understanding while developing their literacy skills. Although some types of poetry are very quick to write and take little classroom time, poetry can also be used as part of a larger class project. The power of mathematical poetry is limitless.

CHAPTER 5

Enhancing Oral Communication Skills With Mathematical Talk

Talking and listening are two aspects of literacy that are often expected to develop naturally without the need for explicit classroom instruction. With all of the demands placed on educators and the constantly looming standardized tests, we often choose to focus our efforts and time elsewhere. After all, children learn to talk and listen quite easily through day-to-day activities prior to ever entering school without any type of direct emphasis on developing those skills. Therefore, when children enter school for the first time, we often focus on immersing them in a variety of texts that are rich and meaningful to build a love of reading and ensure that they have the opportunity to listen to stories as part of learning to read.

Also, for the very youngest ages, we encourage invented or temporary spelling and have students dictate their oral thoughts to us, so we can foster reading and writing skills. Why would we need to teach students those skills when most students already come to school with the ability to talk and listen? Talking and listening are two of the most commonly used skills in the outside world. Every day we spend far more time talking and listening than we do reading and writing. It seems only natural to use the tools children already possess to create activities in the classroom that will help build upon those strengths.

Speaking in an articulate manner is required to thrive in the world and be considered literate. Therefore, it is essential to help children become comfortable with orally expressing their ideas. IRA and NCTE recognize the importance of public speaking and include it in the English language arts standards (1996). Students must be able to adjust their spoken language according to their audience and purpose and develop an understanding and respect for those who use language patterns and dialects that differ from their own. (See Standards 4, 9, and 12 in Appendix A for more details.)

The National Center for Education and the Economy joined with the University of Pittsburgh's Learning Research and Development Center to draft standards strongly urging teachers to develop students' oral language skills (Hoff, 2001). To nurture these skills, students must have a wide range of experiences, which builds their self-confidence and helps them share their ideas with various audiences. Talking is a valuable tool that students bring to the classroom. In fact, researchers have shown that many students use drawing and talking to organize their understanding of the world around them (Dyson, 1989). Although even very young children can talk, many children, and even some adults, have trouble with different types of speaking. Many people aren't comfortable expressing their thoughts to groups of people or strangers, and many would rather avoid public speaking altogether. This is due in part to the fact that within the educational context, we often don't build on the natural abilities that students bring to school. Instead of refining those skills, we expect them to continue developing naturally through life experiences.

Along with talking, listening is the other aspect of literacy that is often ignored in the curriculum. Although many children have the ability to hear, they need focused and varied activities to develop listening skills. Haven't we all read a student's paper and discovered that the student's response had nothing to do with what we asked? We all know people who claim to have selective hearing, but perhaps they never really mastered the art of listening. In a complex society, we must learn to listen to understand and appreciate other points of view and expand our own knowledge base.

Social language and academic language are two very different types of language use. Often academic language is less familiar, and the language patterns and vocabulary are very different from those found in daily social language. This is especially true for ELs. Students may be comfortable when speaking with friends and family, but academic talk may be difficult for them. We must take the vocabulary words that students need to learn and teach these words within the content area and context. As educators are well aware, isolated sheets of vocabulary words are not the way to foster academic language (Au, 1993). In fact, Cazden (2005) challenges educators to modify their current practices to incorporate more academic language. One way to expand the academic language is to create literacy–mathematics connections.

In this chapter, we discuss the various types of listening that children need to develop, then we examine the types of mathematical talk we want to encourage in the classroom. Accompanying the discussion of mathematical talk are specific oral language activities that can be connected easily through mathematics. Guidelines are provided to help educators assess their own classroom's use of oral communication. Finally, we take a look at important considerations when developing talking and listening in the classroom. Many of the activities in this chapter can be modified for different grade levels. As teachers try out some of the ideas and share them with colleagues, even more ideas can be generated. I hope that these suggestions help teachers rethink and reassess their own current practices in the classroom to determine if there are modifications that can be made to activities already used to enhance oral language growth.

Listening in the Classroom

When we refer to oral language development, talking is only half of the equation. To enhance our oral language skills, we must learn to be effective listeners. Talking and listening are closely related and tend to develop together. According to Wolvin and Coakley (1996), not all listening is the same. These researchers believe we listen either discriminatively, aesthetically, efferently, or critically, according to our purpose. Therefore, it is important that students know our expectations and have a clear purpose for listening; we need to know exactly what we are asking our students to do when we want them to listen. Let's look at how the four types of listening might be developed in a mathematical lesson.

Discriminative Listening

This type of listening requires more than just the ability to discriminate among sounds to decode words. Discriminative listening is used by children to understand nonverbal behavior. Adults must be able to read nonverbal cues in order to understand social interaction fully. Recognizing and comprehending nonverbal behavior is a skill that must be learned. Students can gain experience recognizing nonverbal behavior through conducting mathematical interviews and learn to discriminate between important and less important information through listening to a variety of mathematical talk, such as oral reports. Students learn very quickly that valued information is often emphasized.

As math lessons are taught, students realize that when teachers orally reread a page during a mathematical trade book talk, point to a chart or visual that shows information, or lean forward when facilitating small groups engaged in focused mathematical talk, the teacher is saying something that is important or the information is valued by the teacher. Students don't necessarily know when a mathematical concept is important, but if the teacher writes it on the board, adds it to a word wall, or repeats the concept, then students realize that the information is something that is important to know. Thus, students realize that important mathematical information is often reinforced through more than just words. Teachers can help develop this type of listening in a variety of ways as students participate in the type of mathematical talk discussed within this chapter.

Aesthetic Listening

Normally students listen aesthetically when they are listening to something for enjoyment. When people forget about the world around them and become immersed in the story world of a book, then they are aesthetically involved with the text (Rosenblatt, 1978). The type of listening used must be appropriate for the type of activity occurring. If students listen to a mathematical trade book to determine an answer to a problem, then aesthetic listening may not be appropriate. When sharing mathematical trade books, however, the texts can be read aloud purely for aesthetic involvement the first time they are introduced to the class. Students can talk about their favorite parts of the book and make intertextual connections.

Efferent Listening

When students listen efferently, they are listening to take away information—that is, listening to learn. Much of what we teach in school requires this type of listening. Students must listen efferently when they listen to mathematical trade books, work in small groups completing activities, follow along as a teacher or classmate explains a flowchart, and review aloud the steps necessary to complete a problem. We can help children listen efferently by explaining the purpose for the activity, keeping the students involved in the activity, and engaging them in either class notes that are written on the board or individual notes that they write down for themselves.

Critical Listening

This is the type of listening that is necessary to understand and evaluate a speaker's viewpoint. When students try to persuade others through a mathematical debate, critical listening is required to evaluate the factual information. This type of listening can also be fostered through other types of formal mathematical talk such as reports and interviews. Critical listening must be developed because, as students listen to commercials on the radio, watch television shows and movies, and attend plays, they should analyze what they hear. Students should try to recognize the factual information to determine the speaker's point of view. Often propaganda techniques are used to change listeners' opinions. To make educated decisions in society, students must learn to critically listen to others, and we can expand the opportunities students have with this type of listening through mathematical talk.

Talking in the Classroom

The types of talk that we may encounter when developing and reinforcing mathematical concepts will vary widely. They can range from informal mathematical conversations to formal presentations and debates. We want students to have a range of talking opportunities in the classroom, and the easiest way to do this is to begin with less threatening types of activities and progress to more formal types of mathematical talk. That doesn't mean that informal mathematical conversations and focused mathematical communication need to end when the formal talk begins. A classroom community will see a variety of talk occurring on a daily basis.

Informal Mathematical Conversations

Mathematical conversations are a type of instructional conversations that stand in sharp contrast to more traditional forms of teaching. In the traditional forms, the teacher will often lecture to impart specific information to the students. However, mathematical conversations are more spontaneous and informal than other types of talk, and students participate in conversations with their peers when they are working in small groups, engaged with hands-on activities, or working on math problems. Students also engage in conversations with the teacher. Mathematical conversations are often the least threatening type of talk and require the smallest amount of preparation by the teacher and students.

Although good instructional conversations might appear to be fairly simple, they require effort from all involved. According to Goldenberg (1992), these conversations are characterized by a high level of involvement, and no one person should dominate the discussion. They play a vital role in students' oral language development. Through listening to our students' conversations with peers and interacting with them, we can better understand what they are thinking and what mathematical misunderstandings they may possess.

In a classroom community, there should be plenty of interesting material about which students want to talk. Local texts that they create can be a motivating source for discussions. Perhaps students can orally expand on ideas that they wrote in a journal entry reflecting on how math is important to them. Maybe they look at a wall chart that shows how many minutes it takes each student to get home from school, notice something on the chart that they hadn't seen before, and mention it to the teacher or a classmate. A small group of students may reread a favorite class-created mathematical trade book or play a favorite math game and share their ideas. These are all valuable conversations.

Teachers can extend students' mathematical responses in class by asking another question that requires an answer. If a student points out something on a mathematical chart or thinks of another way to solve a problem, the teacher might ask the student how he or she figured that out or even ask the student to explain the finding to a classmate. Listening and expanding on student comments not only help show the students that we are interested in what they are saying but also encourage the development of oral language skills. The student then will think at a higher level and develop a solid understanding of the mathematical content. By asking why students chose to complete a problem in a certain way or how the problem might be approached differently, we require them not only to think at a higher level but also to be able to articulate and communicate these mathematical thoughts.

We can easily connect these mathematical conversations into the home. Students fluent in a language not primarily spoken in the classroom may be allowed to take a mathematical trade book home in their first language to share with their family. This helps connect the families and the school and gives the child additional exposure to the trade book while rereading and discussing it with a family member. Standard 10 of the English language arts standards encourages teachers to allow ELs to use their first language to foster an understanding of content area material (IRA & NCTE, 1996; see Appendix A).

As community facilitators, teachers play a key role in these conversations. For students to have these conversations, it is vital to create a classroom community where students understand that everyone deserves to be treated with respect. Students need support and encouragement from their peers, and they need to be able to share their own ideas without being overshadowed by more outspoken classmates. It is important to help students understand that they must encourage, respect, and care about their peers (Boyce, Alber-Morgan, & Riley, 2007). Although it takes time to create a community of learners, it is important for the classroom climate throughout the year. Research has shown (Galda, Bisplinghoff, Pellegrini, & Stahl, 1995) that a sense of community is critical to a classroom. Even though conversations are often viewed as a low-risk, nonthreatening form of talk, that is unfortunately not true for all students. Some need additional encouragement to share their views and ideas, and the teacher can play a key role in fostering that dialogue. In the sections that follow, two types of activities using mathematical conversations are presented.

Mathematical Trade Book Talk. Mathematical trade books are often the focus of a great deal of discussion in the classroom. When talking about a book, the teacher is reinforcing the idea that comprehension is the purpose of reading. Students can discuss the illustrations and the text. If the book is a storybook, then the students can make predictions, discuss the plot, and even have think-alouds about the material that is being read. When students get confused, the teacher can direct them to reread the text, just as would be done with any trade book. All of this talk helps students understand the text and develop speaking and listening skills. The discussion will allow students to build background knowledge as they share experiences that relate to the book. Teachers can extend student comments to further increase the learning. Sharing mathematical trade books increases academic vocabulary as students hear and see words specific to the mathematical content area.

Reading aloud from children's literature is also an excellent way for ELs to develop both comprehension and vocabulary skills (Hickman, Pollard-Durodola, & Vaughn, 2004). Research supports the importance of developing oral language skills by encouraging discussions and interactions with texts (Au, 1993). Sharing mathematical trade books can enhance all students' oral language abilities as well as improve their comprehension skills and knowledge of mathematical concepts.

Circle Discussions. Many kindergarten and first-grade teachers begin their days with circle time—a sharing time when all students are invited to discuss. Specifically, this can be used as a time to have students talk about something they remember learning the day before in mathematics. The group might use a cube or another geometric shape to designate the speaker, then the person sharing information holds the shape. When the speaker is done, the shape is passed to another student who has something to share. Students also can talk about how they used mathematics at home the night before or even that morning. Students may not realize that they use mathematics within minutes of waking up when they or their parents look at the clock to see the time. Lots of interesting mathematical conversations can be held during circle discussions.

Focused Mathematical Communication

Focused mathematical communication refers to a more formal type of talk than the spontaneous conversations that students might have with one another or with the teacher. With this type of communication, the children clearly have a task that they want to achieve and a goal to meet. Most mathematical activities require this type of talk. Focused mathematical communication is less spontaneous than a conversation on a mathematical topic, but it is less formal than formal mathematical talk. The activities that follow are popular reading strategies that easily tie into mathematics and can be extremely beneficial for developing oral language skills.

Concept Circles. Concept circles were originally developed by Vacca, Vacca, and Gove (1987) and have also been referred to as powerful pyramids and mystery squares, depending on the shape used. When applied to mathematics, this activity can help students think about relationships and categories. For math use, I simply refer to these shapes as math mysteries. Because there may be more than one correct answer for the problem or perhaps one answer that is better than other possible answers, the real value in solving math mysteries lies in the explanations that students orally provide. Students must be able to clearly explain their reasoning for the solution they chose to complete the math mystery. This helps students think about relationships among the mathematical concepts. Math mysteries can be completed with no discussion, but the teacher would lose the oral language benefits of this activity. Without discussion, the mysteries become more of an assessment or a worksheet to complete instead of a puzzle to be solved, and the activity loses a lot of its educational value.

Math mysteries can be used in a variety of ways, and the difficulty level of the shapes can vary. Figure 1 shows three different levels of math mysteries that might be used with students. Figure 1A shows the most basic kind, in which students need to determine the relationship among four concepts shown in different parts of the shape and write a title for the shape. In this example, students should title the mystery "coins" or "money." Since math mysteries are orally shared, classmates can discuss the manner in which they narrowed the possibilities and their reasoning behind selecting their final answer. Although this example is pretty straightforward, Figures 1B and 1C lend themselves to diverse answers.

Figure 1B is slightly more difficult than Figure 1A. Instead of trying to determine the relationship between three concepts, students must look at a shape that contains a concept that doesn't belong. Although the square, octagon, triangle, and rectangle are all shapes, the instructions tell the students to determine which one doesn't belong. Then they must come up with a title for the shape that demonstrates the relationship among the remaining concepts in the triangle. To complete Figure 1B, students must analyze all of the shapes listed. Although there might be a variety of answers for the mystery, one possible answer is to color in the octagon section and title the sample "basic shapes." Another possible answer would be "shapes with an even number of sides."

Figure 1. Three Levels of Math Mysteries

A. Write a title on the line showing the relationship of the terms.

quarter	nickel
dime	penny

_____
Title

B. Color in the section that doesn't belong. Then write a title on the line.

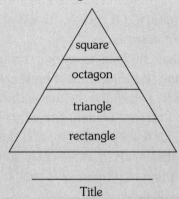

_____
Title

C. Draw a line through the equation that doesn't belong. Replace it with a mathematical equation that makes sense. Put a title on the line.

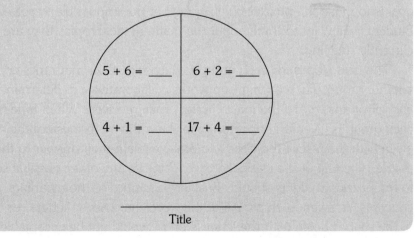

_____
Title

Teachers can let groups work on a math mystery similar to this one, then have the groups explain to the class how their answers were determined. Alternatively, teachers can make many different modifications to this activity. Students might be told the title for the shape and then told to cross out the section that doesn't belong. However, if the exercise is modified in this manner, then there may be only one correct answer, which will dramatically decrease the classroom discussion that ensues.

The most difficult type of math mystery is seen in Figure 1C, in which students must not only determine which section doesn't belong but also replace that concept with one that makes sense. With this sample, students might draw a line through "6 + 2 = _____," then replace it with "6 + 7 = _____ ." They might then create a title such as "problems with answers that are odd numbers." Of course, "6 + 2 = _____" can be replaced with a number of equations.

Teachers can allow their students to work in small groups to solve math mysteries. In the beginning, examples might be shared with the entire class. As a class, the students can determine the answer and orally talk about the method they used to find the solution. Sometimes students have more than one correct answer for a specific shape, and this is an excellent time to let the students know that math mysteries may sometimes have multiple answers. The important thing to remember is that students should orally articulate how the answer is determined.

The students can then be divided into smaller groups. Each group should create a math mystery for another group to solve. The students' goal is to make the puzzles challenging but not impossible to solve. Students will want to think about the mathematical topics they are currently studying.

The next step is for each group to exchange their math mystery with another group. Then each group works collaboratively to determine the answer or answers to the math mystery they received. When time is up, each group is given an opportunity to share the math mystery they were given with the rest of the class and orally explain their answer to the puzzle. The rest of the class can try to think of any other possible solutions to the puzzle. Students should consider semantics or the meanings of the concepts. Answers such as "All of the words have seven letters" or "Three of the shapes begin with the letter *R* or *T*" would not be acceptable. The group that created the puzzle then shares whether the answer is acceptable. Students enjoy the puzzle-like format, which makes math seem more like a game. The teacher may later hang the puzzles up in the classroom on a math mystery wall.

Math mysteries are inexpensive and not time intensive to create. They have a lot of flexibility in the manner in which they might be used in the classroom. In fact, they can be created for almost any mathematical concept that students are learning. Math mysteries can be a great activity to use with small groups of students and can be used in a center where students work with partners during free time. Teachers can vary the difficulty level of the mysteries created and organize them in such a manner that students select a specific color of envelope or paper based on the mathematical difficulty level. Students can take a pack of math mysteries to complete with a peer, then orally discuss with their partner or other group members how they would determine the answer to the mystery. Since some mysteries may have more than one answer, students need to articulate their thoughts and listen carefully to their partner's explanation. When students have free time during the day, they can use their skills to create new puzzles to add to the class collection of math mysteries.

This activity is easy to extend into the home. As long as clear descriptions are provided, the puzzles can be taken home by students to share with their families. The families might even discuss the puzzles and develop other possible solutions for the students to share with the class.

Concept of Definition. Concept of definition is a type of semantic mapping originally developed by Schwartz and Raphael (1985) to help students determine the meaning of a word from context clues. The original purpose was to have students read a chunk of text with an unknown word in it, then figure out the meaning of the word by looking at the context. Students compare the term to a similar concept, think about its category, list several characteristics of it, and finally share some samples. Then they can read the definition they created for the word. Demonstrating relationships through activities like semantic mapping has proven to be very valuable for ELs in particular (Nagy, 1988). Thinking about the relationship among the concepts can help children remember vocabulary.

I prefer to modify this strategy to help students develop an understanding of broad mathematical concepts, which works well with topics such as the metric system, estimating, and even the concept of angles. Instead of reading a chunk of text to determine a meaning, we create a definition based on everything we know about the topic. This strategy works well as a whole-class activity and helps students think about semantic relationships among terms. When the definition is created, the teacher may choose to write it on a chart to display in the classroom, so the students will not only develop oral language but also will have a public local text to which they can refer.

Teachers may want to divide the entire class into small groups and have each group complete a concept of definition chart. Since the students work in groups to brainstorm their knowledge about the topic, a lot of focused mathematical talk can occur. With small groups, there is often a lot more talk than would be evident with a large-group activity. At the end of the activity, a representative from each small group can orally share the group's definition with the rest of the class.

One third-grade teacher was working with a small group of students: Dominique, Vincent, and Talia. All three were receiving extra help because they were struggling with mathematics. The teacher wanted to reinforce the meaning of parallel lines. Together the teacher and students completed part of the chart on the individual students' sheets. They all wrote the term discussed, explained what it was, and compared it to a term that was familiar. Then each student individually listed examples of parallel lines in the world around them, drew pictures to represent what they wrote to reinforce their ideas, and explained when the term was used. Figure 2 shows the concept of definition chart created by Dominique.

After the students each finished their individual concept of definition chart, the teacher led a discussion and encouraged them to orally share their ideas for the different parts of the chart. This important step helped clarify their thinking. Dominique wrote "driving" as a use for parallel lines. When the teacher asked her to explain what she was thinking, Dominique said she was referring to the lines on a road. Also, Vincent and Talia orally explained the phrases they wrote on their charts. This helped the students orally articulate their thoughts and showed the teacher that the children understood the concept.

Venn Diagrams. Venn diagrams help illustrate relationships among concepts. Although originally designed for use in mathematics, many

Figure 2. Student's Concept of Definition Chart for Parallel Lines

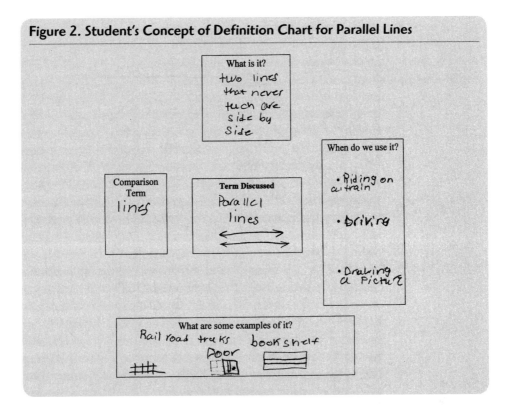

What is it?

two lines that never tuch are side by side

Comparison Term

lines

Term Discussed

Parallel lines

When do we use it?

• Riding on a train

• driving

• Drawing a Picture

What are some examples of it?

Rail road trucks   book shelf
        Door

elementary teachers are familiar with using Venn diagrams as a reading strategy. Teachers can ask students to compare two stories or characters to determine the commonalities and differences between the two. Although Venn diagrams may be familiar to many teachers, I would be doing a disservice if I didn't highlight the strategy in this chapter. The use of Venn diagrams requires a minimum of preparation time by the teacher, yet the activity offers many benefits. This strategy provides an excellent opportunity to develop students' oral language skills as well as mathematical skills.

In Figure 3, we see a second-grade student's comparison of two shapes. From this example, it is obvious that there are many differences between a cube and a cylinder. In the Venn diagram, the student discusses that they do not look the same and have different numbers of vertices and

Figure 3. Student's Venn Diagram Comparing Two Shapes

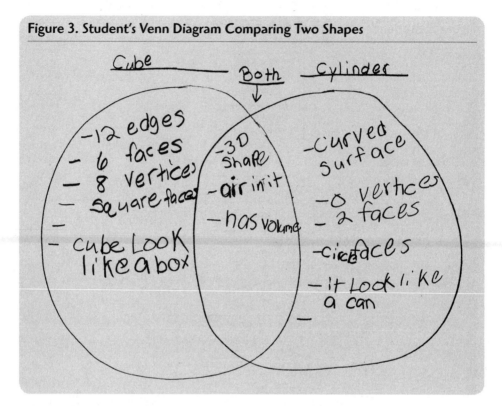

faces. Similarities are also noted: A cube and a cylinder are both three-dimensional shapes and have volume.

Although this student learned a lot by completing the Venn diagram and orally talking about it with the teacher and classmates, the teacher can expand the activity even further. When students are allowed to work in groups to create Venn diagrams, they have to articulate their thoughts, synthesize their peers' ideas, compare and contrast concepts, and use higher level thinking. To really challenge students, teachers may even have small groups compare three different concepts with three overlapping circles. Although Venn diagrams have been used for years, their potential for enhancing literacy skills warrants discussion.

Knowledge Ratings. Teachers can use knowledge ratings to talk about various mathematical concepts and check students' level of understanding of the terms. This activity has been suggested as an alternate to the vocabulary notebooks that some teachers have their students create (Blachowicz, 1986). When this strategy was first developed, teachers listed terms to be learned down the left-hand side of a piece of paper. Across the top of the page, the teacher wrote column headings: "???," "have seen/ heard the term," and "can define the term." Then the students determined individually their level of knowledge for each term in the left-hand column and marked an X in the appropriate column. With this activity, discussion is critical for the activity to retain its value.

One issue is that students may think that they know a mathematical term when in fact they are thinking of a different term. Discussion allows any misunderstandings to be corrected and allows students with prior knowledge of different terms to help others. Also, the talk will help get the concepts into the students' speaking vocabulary. However, a few students who want to impress the teacher may not want to admit that they have never heard the term and may mark a much higher knowledge rating of the terms than they actually possess. Therefore, this strategy works best as a means of getting students talking about terms. Let them know that this activity is not going to be collected and graded. The goal is to self-assess their level of knowledge about each term, then discuss what they know as a class.

I prefer to modify this strategy from the original design. Rating often insinuates that there is some type of judgment being made. Instead, I ask students to "tell us what you know!" Teachers may have students draw a line through the terms they don't know, then see if they can explain, draw a picture of, and give an example of the terms they do know. One teacher used this with a class of first graders, who were reviewing geometry and shapes they had learned.

Figure 4 is Quentin's sheet. He drew a smiley face in each of the first two columns when he remembered hearing a word or thought he could explain it. Some students left boxes blank because they hadn't heard of the word or couldn't explain it, but Quentin thought he knew all of the words. In the third column, students were asked to draw a picture of the shape. In the last box, they were asked what the shape looked like, which gave them the opportunity to draw a picture of where they had seen the shape in everyday life. This was an excellent way to have them think about math outside the classroom context.

Figure 4. Student's "Tell Us What You Know!" Sheet Containing Math Concepts

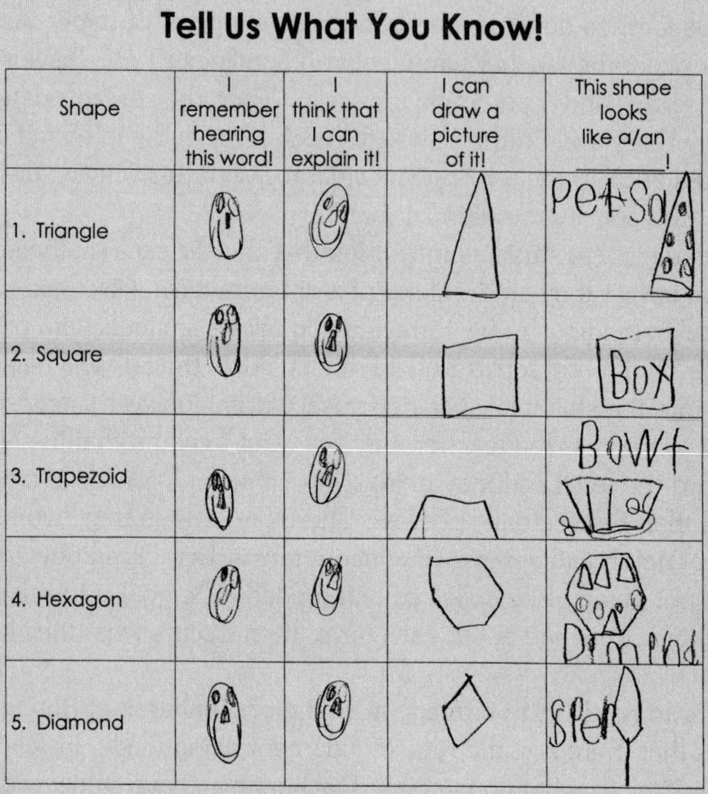

Tell Us What You Know!

Shape	I remember hearing this word!	I think that I can explain it!	I can draw a picture of it!	This shape looks like a/an ____!
1. Triangle				PetSa
2. Square				Box
3. Trapezoid				Bowt
4. Hexagon				Dimnd
5. Diamond				Sper

Similar to the original version of knowledge rating, the students still showed their level of understanding. Obviously it is a pretty low level of understanding if a student can only remember hearing a word and only slightly better if the student can explain it. However, it requires a much higher level of thinking not only to know what the term is but also to draw a picture and apply the mathematical term to real life. The class talked about each of the words after completing their sheets, which enabled some students who could not remember the words not only to develop an understanding of the term but also to see a variety of ways the concept was evident in the world. The benefit of this activity is the oral discussion of each word. To complete the activity, students are required to think about their level of understanding for each concept. They are learning a lot from listening to the classroom discussion and gaining ideas from classmates.

List-Group-Label. This strategy is one of my favorites to use with a group of students. Originally it was designed as a prereading strategy (Taba, 1967) for content areas such as science and social studies. However, it can also help students categorize items and discriminate among concepts in a variety of content areas, including mathematics. As a whole-class activity, the students brainstorm a list of items that they think of when they hear a certain topic. For third- through sixth-grade classes, teachers might ask the students to brainstorm 20–25 terms. If teachers wish to use this activity with younger grades, it may be easier to use a smaller number of words, depending on the ages and ability levels present in the class. Working in small groups, students must decide which words have something in common and list those in a group. The students must then write a title for the group of words that illustrates the words' relationship. It is important to emphasize that words can be used in more than one group.

It is always interesting the way different groups of students choose to categorize words. Working collaboratively with other group members, the students can build off one another's ideas and knowledge, which are shared orally to create the categories. I encourage students to try to keep word categories to four to six words. If a group of terms is too large, then perhaps the students can look at the terms in that group to further discriminate among the concepts and divide the group into multiple groups. This creates quite a bit of discussion, and the children have to really think about the similarities and differences among the terms. After the small groups categorize all of the terms, I ask each group to share their most interesting category and the title they chose for it.

A third-grade teacher who decided to use this activity asked her class to brainstorm a list of terms related to math, and the students came up with 29 words. The teacher then chorally read through the list with the students to make sure they could read all of the terms. As each term was read, the teacher had a student explain the mathematical concept. Then she typed and photocopied the list of words, so her students could cut out the words and then place them in groups.

Later in the day, each student worked with a partner to categorize the math terms. A variety of categories were created by the different pairings of students. While one pair created a category titled math signs, another group decided to have a category called answer signs. Categories such as fraction words and graph words were also created by some groups. For this activity, the teacher had the students cut out the terms and glue them in categories on large sheets of paper. If this is done, it is important to give students extra copies of the list, so that terms can be glued in more than one category.

It is vital that students have the opportunity to share their category creations orally. Although some of the categories created were interesting, it is only through discussion that the teacher will realize the students' thinking for each term. By orally sharing ideas for some of the categories, students are not only thinking about complex relationships among mathematical terms but also are required to articulate their thoughts.

"I Have _____. Who Has _____?" This game is very popular with teachers of all levels. It was originally designed to build sight word vocabulary, but over the years I have met a number of teachers who enjoy using it with mathematical concepts. Whenever I introduce it in class or at a presentation, I always have some teachers who have not been exposed to it yet are eager to try it with their students. "I have _____. Who has _____?" is a game that can be adapted for use from kindergarten through middle school. Students love it and often ask to play the game again, and other teachers report similar results. Each student receives a card created by the teacher with the following two sentences on it:

I have _____.
Who has _____?

A different vocabulary word is written in each blank, such that only one student has a word in the first blank of their card that matches one other student's word in the second blank of their card. The student with the first card starts the game by reading the card to the rest of the class. The student who has the answer to the question on the card read goes next.

If a kindergarten teacher wants to reinforce the spellings of different numerals, the teacher may create cards with the number words on them (e.g., one, two, three). The game begins when the student who has the "I have <u>one</u>. Who has <u>two</u>?" card reads it aloud, then the student who has the "I have <u>two</u>. Who has <u>three</u>?" card reads next. The game continues until the last card is read. When I do this activity in class, I like to have the last card with only the phrase "I have _____." written on it, so I can conclude the game.

This game can easily be modified to reinforce academic language by writing vocabulary terms like acute triangle, rectangle, and rhombus on the cards. The first card in a series of cards designed to reinforce shape terms may be, "I have <u>a circle</u>. Who has <u>a shape with four equal sides</u>?" Then the next card might read "I have <u>a square</u>. Who has <u>a shape with eight equal sides</u>?"

Other teachers like to play the game as a fun way to review a certain computational skill that the students are learning. Cards in a set like this might be "I have <u>4</u>. Who has <u>42 divided by 2</u>?" and "I have <u>21</u>. Who has <u>12 divided by 2</u>?" Of course, these cards could be used for much more difficult computations with older students.

Regardless of the age or ability level, this game provides an opportunity to review skills with a minimum of instructional time in preparation and in usage. For those small time periods when teachers often turn to "sponge" activities, this is a great way to make use of the time. Although the activity would lose the oral language benefits, these cards can even be included in a small-group activity. Students can work in pairs to arrange the cards in order, then use a self-checking sheet to see if they have the answers correct.

"Got It!" This mathematical review activity helps students get over their phobia of math word problems by asking them to create their own. The teacher puts a number of cards in a can or box. On each card are two numbers. Also, there should be several "sorry" cards in the can. Students sit in a circle and one pulls a card out of the can. The student silently reads the two numbers on the card, then creates a word problem that makes sense. For example, if the numbers six and two were on a card, the student might say, "One day I saw six girls walking to school. Two of those girls had on tennis shoes. How many girls didn't have on tennis shoes?" Everyone listens to the word problem and tries to determine the answer.

If the student who created the word problem was able to create a problem that makes sense, the student gets to keep the card. Everyone has to listen carefully to make sure the problem makes sense and see if they can figure out the answer. Without repeating the problem, the next person in the circle tries to solve the problem in a complete sentence. In this case, the solver might say, "Four girls didn't have on tennis shoes." If the class determines that the answer is correct, the student who solved the problem gets to pull a card from the can and make up a new problem. If a student pulls a sorry card from the can, all of the cards that that student collected must go back in the can. Therefore, the student who wins isn't automatically the strongest math student—there is an element of luck involved. The purpose of the activity is not necessarily to see which students are the strongest at math but to provide students with an enjoyable way to get additional practice at word problems.

This activity can easily be modified to be more challenging. Students might pull out cards that have three numbers on them and have to create a word problem with all three. For example, if a student pulled a card with a five, three, and two on it, the student might say, "There are five flower beds. Each flower bed has three flowers in it, and on each flower there are two bees. How many bees are there?" The answer is "There are 30 bees." The teacher may choose to let students have a notepad or dry erase board to jot down the numerical problem that the students create. The students might even be asked to create a picture to show how to solve the problem, then several students might share their drawings with the rest of the class.

Trivia Hunt. Like many adults, students are often fascinated with trivia. To expand mathematical knowledge, we can capitalize on this natural inquisitiveness by asking trivia questions. One idea is for a teacher to have a math trivia box, and as time permits, the students can try to answer questions in the box. Then students can research in books or on the Internet and talk to other people they know to try to determine the answer. Trivia teams can brainstorm the best sources they might use to determine the answer and then divide up the resources to search. Students gain more information by conducting the research than just getting the correct answer. In the process of looking for the solution, students will more than likely read about other interesting information, which will expand their mathematical background.

On a set day, teams can meet again to share what they found and determine if they can come to a consensus. Then each team can write down their best guess and share it with the rest of the class. After answering the question, the class might even discuss any additional mathematical information that they learned in the process. Furthermore, students will enjoy researching and creating their own trivia questions for the box for the rest of the class to try to answer. Finally, this activity is a great way to incorporate exit slips (see Chapter 3) for the students to reveal one interesting fact about math that they learned during the process.

The following represent some of the mathematical trivia facts that students might find interesting:

- How did the term *acre* get its name?
- What is an abacus? Where was it created? Does anyone still use it?
- What is a google? Why do they call it that?
- What is a baker's dozen, and why do we use that phrase?
- What is the legend behind how tangrams were named?

Math trivia is a game that has many benefits beyond oral language development, such as providing writing practice, enhancing research skills, and encouraging students to work together as a team. Within the English language arts standards, Standards 7 and 8 pertain specifically to research (IRA & NCTE, 1996; see Appendix A). While Standard 7 focuses on students' ability to generate questions and ideas that require research, Standard 8 focuses on students' ability to use a variety of resources, including technological ones, to gather information. Both the ability to generate questions that can be answered and the ability to conduct research by gathering information are important. Trivia hunt is an activity that can help students meet the English language arts standards and expand their own mathematical understanding.

Formal Mathematical Talk

Formal mathematical talk is often the most difficult type of talk for many people because it requires presenting or talking with others in a less spontaneous manner than mathematical conversations or focused mathematical communication. This type of talk requires the speaker to spend time preparing the oral presentation beforehand and then share the information or presentation with a group. All of us at some point in our lives have been in the uncomfortable situation of having to make a speech or presentation and experiencing the sweaty palms and racing heart.

Each formal talk situation is different. The audience, the level of knowledge we have about the topic, and the amount of speaking experience we have will all influence how comfortable we are with the situation. The interesting thing is that people often expect teachers to get up in front of groups and speak easily. After all, teachers speak in front of their students every day. However, the classroom is a safe and familiar community for teachers, where they feel comfortable with their level of knowledge. I don't need to tell many teachers that there is a world of difference between making a speech to a room of strangers and spending 30 minutes in front of students in the classroom. Students have even less experience in front of groups than do teachers. We want to be sure to make these initial formal talk activities positive experiences because negative experiences will likely make future public speaking even harder for students.

Experiencing a formal talk activity in the classroom can be a valuable use of time for the students; the goal is to look at the entire process. What can we do to create a formal talk activity that will provide the greatest student benefits? We want a process that entails a great deal of talk and from which the children can learn. Students who spend hours creating the background for a play and just a short period of time practicing and presenting their creation are not getting the educational benefits they deserve from the formal talk activity.

Moving Students From Informal Conversations to Formal Mathematical Talk. During the first few months of the elementary school year, there may be a lot of mathematical conversations and focused mathematical communication. While that is occurring, a sense of community is developing. At this time it is important to establish with the class the qualities of a good listener. Students need to know how to help others feel more at ease when they are talking. The next step is to plan group presentations so that students have the security and assistance of other group members.

In the lower elementary grades, teachers may want to do only small-group presentations unless a student wants to make a formal presentation. However, I have found that the youngest students are often the most self-confident when it comes to talking to a group of peers. The goal is not to create a classroom of salesmen or future presidential hopefuls but rather to help students be able to articulate their ideas and messages in a clear, confident manner. Those oral language skills are required in the world in which we live, and we want to help prepare students for that world.

The following plan represents one way that mathematical talk may occur during a typical year. Of course, the activities will vary depending on the age level of the students and the oral language experiences with which they have been involved. As shown through the activities discussed, the idea is to start with the least threatening type of talk in the classroom, then continue to build upon the skills developed to reach more formal types of talk. The schedule can vary widely, depending on the needs of the students. Some individual activities could even be completed in pairs so that the students can provide support to each other as necessary. Teachers working as facilitators in oral language development must decide when students are ready to move onto the next level.

In the early fall, students spontaneously engage with others in mathematical conversations about trade books and local texts that they see in the classroom. Teachers extend those conversations and help students explain their thoughts. During this time, students will work together in small groups to discuss and figure out problems with math manipulatives. During circle time, they might share different ways that mathematics ties into their home and community or new math concepts they are learning. This circle time dialogue may include contributions they bring from home to share that show the math connection outside the classroom walls.

As students become comfortable with the previously mentioned activities, they will want to present in groups a mathematical chart that they created. Taking turns, one student can share a fact in the chart, and then another student might encourage a listener in the class to ask the group a question. When parents or visitors come by, students can volunteer to share and talk about public mathematical texts in the classroom. Students take turns sharing group information with the rest of the class as they complete group activities like concept of definition, list-group-label, and concept circles.

By this point, students should feel more at ease with orally sharing information. They have listened to a number of mathematical trade books that present a problem for the reader to solve. Together the students can work in groups to create a skit about a story that they wrote, which may require the listener to solve a mathematical problem using recently learned mathematical skills. The teacher may have students share and discuss a mathematical trade book with another class. Often students are more comfortable presenting to younger students.

Finally, students are ready for formal presentations. They may share their mathematical knowledge with other classes and those outside the school setting. This might even involve sharing with classmates at their level or older. Also, students will be ready to play an active role in parent nights. The teacher can even have a special mathematical literacy night for the students to showcase the mathematical concepts they are learning. The following section outlines additional types of formal mathematical talk.

Debates. When students conduct debates, they learn how to use oral language to persuade others. They have to provide facts and information that listeners will understand. Debates can easily tie into mathematics. As a class, students may debate why their class should receive more or less time in mathematics during the school day or the importance of mathematics and why more money should be spent on calculators and other items for math class.

Even younger students can successfully participate in debates with appropriate scaffolding. The teacher may introduce debates by having the class brainstorm as a group the pros and cons of a topic. As ideas are mentioned, they are listed on a board or large sheet of paper divided into two columns. Then the teacher explains to the students that often there are two different views on a topic; debates are a great opportunity to share those views and explain them. A new topic is selected, and each student decides whether to come up with a pro or con idea to write on a piece of paper to share with the class. If this is too difficult for younger students, they may work in pairs to come up with the idea or draw a picture to represent the thought they wish to share.

Math may even be tied into debates on topics that are not normally associated with mathematics. Almost any debate can be enhanced by asking students to research statistics and data that support their point of view. Students may create visual representations, such as graphs and charts, to share information for their debate. The following are just a few ideas that students might debate:

- Mathematics instructional time should be lengthened.
- Students should be allowed to use calculators on tests.
- Schools will save money by closing down on Fridays.
- Recycling is a good idea.
- Students do not need math class next year.
- All countries need a common measurement system.

One sixth-grade class decided to debate whether students should be required to take mathematics after sixth grade. The class discussed the idea of a debate and watched a brief video on public speaking found on the Internet. Then the students were given two minutes to individually create a pro list for being required to enroll in a math class the next year and then another two minutes to brainstorm a con list. The class orally shared their responses, then created a class list together. As the teacher wrote their ideas on an overhead transparency, the students were invited to use their classmates' ideas to modify their own.

After developing the lists, the teacher then created a scenario where someone was accused of a crime, and she asked the students to think about what type of evidence would be needed to prove innocence or guilt. They discussed that each side in a debate needs evidence and must try to persuade others to their way of thinking. The teacher then talked about the importance of oral language in relation to debates. The students shared that it was important that both sides take turns and that people shouldn't interrupt others who are sharing their point of view. After that, students chose sides for the debate.

The next step was to research information for the debate. Students worked individually and reviewed an article and a website to find facts they could write down to support their side of the debate. Students then organized their facts on index cards so that each student would have something to contribute to the debate. Both groups selected individuals to be responsible for making opening and closing statements for the debate.

Once the students were prepared, it was time to set up the physical aspects of the classroom for the debate. The furniture was organized so that the debate groups faced each other. The area was designed for students to sit no more than two feet apart, so that they could easily hear and be engaged in listening while others shared information.

Then it was time for the debate. Again, the value was not only in the actual presentation but also in the entire process leading up to the debate. Students learned to consider the purpose, audience, and format when conducting their research. In addition, they had to organize their writing to articulate their views on the topic clearly. Finally, during the debate, they practiced their oral speaking and listening skills to help share their perspective.

Afterward, students reflected on the debate by writing down the aspects of the debate that they enjoyed and those they disliked. Also, they related whether they would like to have classroom debates in the future. Looking through the written reflections, most students described the debate as "fun" and wanted to do it again. Many mentioned that they enjoyed learning exactly how to debate and that it gave them the opportunity to "speak their minds" and say what they thought on the topic.

Even though many students might not be eager to do research, these students seemed to find conducting research an interesting task because it had an authentic purpose to support their side in the debate. Chanyce said, "I like when we had to gather information for the debate because we had to be like real detectives." Several students not only enjoyed the debate but also had ideas for other topics they could debate in the future. Janay wrote, "I would like to do another debate on should you go to collage yes or no? because you can learn more about collage." Student enthusiasm is evident in responses like Ashanti's, who said she loved it and wrote that she decided that she "might become a lawyer."

Because this was the first time the students had participated in a debate, it wasn't surprising that many didn't like that multiple students sometimes tried to talk at the same time. Also, some students wanted more time to meet with their group to plan their presentation. However, LeAndra best summed up the teacher and students' view on debating when she wrote, "I would like to do it again because it was fun and we would probably do better the second time that we debate." Math may even be tied into debates on topics that are not normally associated with mathematics. Almost any debate can be enhanced by asking students to research statistics and data to support their point of view on a subject. Then students may create visual representations, such as graphs and charts, to share information in their debate.

Interviews. Interviews are an excellent way to develop both speaking and listening skills. Many students have seen interviews on television and the Internet; therefore, it is quite easy to show students that this activity uses language for an authentic purpose and ties to the world beyond the classroom. Although students have probably seen interviews, it does not mean that they can conduct one effectively, as it requires excellent oral language skills. However, similar to other types of mathematical talk, younger students can successfully participate in interviews. The teacher will want to consider the ability levels and ages of the students, but with modifications, even the lower grade levels can be introduced to interviewing. If the students are very young, the teacher may choose to have the entire class interview someone while the teacher records the answers on a large sheet of paper.

The first step is to have students observe actual interviews. Showing students a few videotaped interviews also helps build their visual literacy skills, which are another important aspect of literacy. To understand interviews, students must comprehend a type of text that is often not written. Prior to viewing interviews, ask students to think about the qualities of an effective interview. Let students brainstorm in groups a possible list of ideas to share with the rest of the class. The person conducting the interview must be enthusiastic and interested in both the content and the person they are interviewing. In addition, eye contact, tone, voice, rate of speech, and pace must be considered. Finally, ask students to analyze the type of questions the interviewer asks the interviewee. Are yes/no questions getting the most interesting responses or do open-ended questions provide more information?

Then explain to the students that they will be conducting interviews. There are many possible mathematical topics that might be considered for the interviews depending on the teacher's and students' preferences. Here are a few ideas:

- Interview parents or other adults on how they learned math in elementary school. Did they use calculators? Did they use computers? What types of text did they use? These types of questions require students to be able to articulate their own mathematical learning and compare and contrast information.

- Ask an adult how math is used in everyday life or at work. This type of interview would reinforce the importance of math in the real world.

- Interview the principal regarding the reasons why it is important for students to learn math.

- Interview a teacher who teaches at the next level to find out the mathematical concepts students will be learning next year, and ask what students can do this year to be ready for math next year.

After the mathematical topic is determined for the interviews, it is time to create the questions. The students may work in small groups to come up with questions, and then as a class decide which questions to use. Before actually practicing the interview questions, it is time to talk about being a good listener. What qualities does a good listener possess? In the role of interviewer, the student must listen efferently so that information is remembered. Furthermore, the person interviewing must monitor comprehension and modify or add questions to clarify the interviewee's response.

Then it is time to try out an interview. Invite a parent, school staff person, or even a community member into the classroom. If that isn't possible, the students might want to visit another class to practice their interviewing skills with those students. Emphasize that key points need to be written down, so the students can remember what was discussed in the interview. They may want to record the interview, so they can listen to it again and jot down ideas they might have missed. After the practice interviews, discuss what was learned and what students will do differently when they complete their next interviews.

Although conducting the interviews has a great deal of value, an important part of the process is prior to and after the interviews (Tompkins, 2009). Bring the students back together as a whole class to discuss what they learned. Was there anything they would do differently? Was anything more difficult than they expected? What did they learn about their mathematical topic? Can the students graph or show the information they gained in some way to share the results with others?

One third-grade teacher decided to have her students conduct an interview about a mathematical concept they were studying. The class began with a discussion about why interviews occur and where they take place. Since governmental elections were held days prior to this discussion, the students had seen a lot of interviews on their televisions at home and were eager to share new knowledge. Students also had prior experience watching interviews on talk shows, sitcoms, and the news. Students realized that newspaper reporters might interview others to get information for articles. The teacher then focused this discussion on a narrower topic related to when students might use interviews to learn about math.

The third-grade teacher explained that they would be interviewing an adult about fractions. Each student brainstormed in their journals a list of questions they might ask. As a class, they shared their ideas, which the teacher listed on an overhead transparency. The class then reviewed what made good questions and decided which ones they wanted to ask, then drew a line through those they didn't want to use. The students then voted on their three favorite questions from the ones remaining in the list. The teacher typed up the winning questions and added two of her own that she thought might be a good idea to ask. Then the students took these final five questions home to interview an adult:

1. What is a fraction?
2. Why do you think fractions are important?
3. How do you use fractions in your everyday life?
4. In what grade did you first learn fractions?
5. Can you make a fraction problem?

The next day the students shared their results with a classroom buddy, and the pairs tried to find similarities among the results. After that, the entire class discussed what they learned. Most of the students interviewed their mothers, but some interviewed fathers, grandparents, and even aunts and older siblings.

The most interesting and varied answers were in response to applying fractions in their daily lives and sharing why fractions were important. The adults had a wide range of ideas. The most common activities mentioned were cooking and baking. However, one father is a carpenter, and he mentioned that he uses fractions in his job and that knowing how to read fractions correctly on prints helps him accurately determine distances. Other specific ideas shared from the interviews included the importance of using fractions to measure hardwood floors and mix hair dye. The students finished the activity by answering two questions themselves: What did you learn from the interviews about fractions? and Why do you think interviews are a good way to learn about math?

Completing these class interviews enabled the students not only to develop oral language skills but also to see the relevance of math in the everyday world. The experience provided the students with an authentic literacy experience because they had a real purpose for asking the questions and writing the answers. Interviewing was an activity with which the students had prior knowledge from watching television, and they knew it was a valued activity for many adults, which made the activity engaging and motivating.

Raps and Plays. Children enjoy trying creative new ways to express their mathematical thoughts and ideas orally. Raps and plays are two types of oral communication that can be particularly popular. Raps are a familiar form of communication to many students, and they enjoy the rhythm found in raps. Plays, on the other hand, are also a great way for students to share mathematical knowledge orally because they have an opportunity to act out a script that they wrote. Because both raps and plays can require extensive preparation from the participants, and the results are often shared with a larger audience, these two types of mathematical talk are categorized in this chapter as formal talk.

One sixth-grade teacher invited her students to create raps or short plays to help other students remember new terms such as *mode, median,* and *mean.* The goal was to explain a specific mathematical concept that the students were learning. Therefore in their creation, they had to include mathematical information. This turned out to be a very popular activity. The boys in the class were especially excited to try to write and present a rap. Connor and Lars wrote the following on the concept of mode:

> The Mode Rap
> The mode is the number in the data that has the most load.
> The way you find the mode is you gotta find the number that accurs the most.
> When you find that that number it will be your host.
> Connor—Drummer
> Lars—Raper

The students enjoyed creating raps and thought it was a fun way for them to reinforce information for other students to remember.

While Connor and Lars chose to create a rap, three other classmates decided they wanted to try writing a play. They knew they wanted to explain a concept related to the metric system and finally decided on explaining meter (the metric unit of length):

Ter: I'm the lonelyest soul on Saturn.

Me: I'm me. I'm the loneliest person on Saturn without a friend named ter.

Narater: Both Me and Ter were very lonely as you can tell.

Narater: Then Me ran into Ter.

Ter: I'm sorry. Oh my name is Ter. Whats ur name?

Me: I'm Me!

            (Me+Ter)

Both Me
and Ter: And together, we're meter, the metric unit of length!

Plays are a difficult genre to write, but the sixth-grade students had the opportunity to learn a lot from the experience. The metric play has three characters, Me, Ter, and the narrator. The students tried to imitate conventions they had seen in previous plays by listing the character speaking on the left-hand side of the page. Although their play is brief, common story elements could be seen in the presentation. The characters are introduced in the beginning, and the authors bring the play to closure by the end. Finally, the students explained a mathematical concept, the meter.

Important Considerations Regarding Talking and Listening

Regardless of the type of talking or listening skills that teachers are helping students develop, there are four important considerations that must be remembered. Each of the guidelines in this section will make the experience more positive.

Articulate Purpose

Teachers should understand their reasons for developing oral language skills and articulate these beliefs to the students. Even though the teacher may have a purpose for an activity, it shouldn't be assumed that students will have the same expectations. If students will be listening to a mathematical trade book or viewing a play or oral report, tell them why they are listening. Is there certain information that they are expected to remember? If students are working in groups, let them know that there is a reason for their mathematical conversations and the outcomes that will occur.

Set Realistic Expectations

Teachers should be realistic with off-task talk. It will occur and should be expected, but most people find that students quickly return to the topic at hand on their own (Daiute, 1989). In addition, even off-task talk can be beneficial to oral language development. If a group of students is remaining off task in their conversations, then the teacher should assume the role of facilitator to help the group return to the topic at hand. Know that a great deal of effort has been made to develop the classroom community and trust in the members of the class to do their part.

Be Flexible

Plan activities and create small groups while considering the needs of the students within the classroom. Monitor them working together and modify the groups as necessary. Sometimes an activity may not go as planned, and the format may need to be changed from a small-group activity to a whole-class lesson or even an independent activity. Use flexible grouping and change the groups depending on the task at hand. This will also give students opportunities to interact with a variety of peers.

Keep Activities Varied

Plan a wide variety of activities to develop oral language skills. In this chapter, a number of strategies for developing students' talking and listening skills are shared, and many other activities can be learned by talking with colleagues and attending professional development opportunities. The more ideas teachers can choose from, the better prepared they will be to develop oral language. Even when there is an activity that students ask to do again, it is important to continue to use a wide variety of ideas. The goal is to develop all types of talking and listening, from casual mathematical conversations to the most formal type of talk.

WHERE DO I GO FROM HERE?

We must develop articulate speaking and discriminating, attentive listening in our students if we want them to be prepared to live and thrive in a social environment. Although Loban's (1976) research stresses the importance of teaching talking and listening, many schools and classrooms still stress reading and writing in day-to-day activities. Oral language development must become a stronger focus of our classrooms if we are to achieve our goal. By integrating oral language activities with mathematics, we can do that.

Teachers must take time to examine their classrooms and determine if oral language skills are being nurtured on a regular basis. Are students engaged in a variety of talking and listening activities? Are these activities woven throughout the different content areas, or are they primarily conducted at specific times of day such as a morning message or show-and-tell? When students work in groups, are they constantly encouraged to assess the role they are playing in the discussions? Perhaps guidelines can be shared, and students might ask themselves the following questions:

- How did I contribute to the discussion? What did I have to add?
- How did I help or encourage other students in my group to share ideas?
- How well did we work together as a team?
- The next time our group meets, what is one thing that I would do differently to improve the discussion?

Finally, teachers should ensure that oral language activities are incorporated and tied into the students' lives beyond the classroom. Students need to realize the importance of developing the ability to talk and listen with a variety of purposes in mind. Students must understand that these are valued skills in society and know that oral language skills will continue to develop similarly to other aspects of literacy.

No longer can we look at the social language of students and believe that is enough. We must realize that academic language is very different and that oral language requires time and effort to develop. Within this chapter, a number of specific strategies for targeting oral language development are shared. However, the enhancement of oral language development can occur in almost any mathematical lesson we teach. The key is not only to be a kid watcher but also to watch our own behaviors and actions to ensure that we are taking advantage of teachable moments to reinforce oral language skills.

CHAPTER 6

Viewing and Visually Representing Mathematical Information

In many elementary classrooms, there really isn't much art in the part of the day we refer to as language arts—at least not visual art. Although students are exposed to illustrations or photographs in picture books and other texts, we can do so much more as educators to infuse viewing and visual representation into our classrooms. If art, drawing, or movies are part of the day, they are seen as add-ons to the existing curriculum. Oftentimes, visuals and drama are not emphasized in the classroom and are only part of classroom activities if extra time is available. Instead, the abilities to comprehend words on a page and communicate thoughts through words are typically more highly valued forms of communication that educators seek to develop in classrooms.

When educators speak about reading and comprehending, it is typically understood that they are referring to printed words. It is assumed that literature, textbooks, basal readers, morning message charts, and other more traditional forms of imported and local texts are what students should be able to read and understand. However, that view of literacy is gradually changing. Flood and Lapp (1998), for example, refer to this focus and prioritization of reading and writing as an irrational loyalty. The written word is no long the only type of text that students need to comprehend to be considered literate. Viewing refers to a much wider range of media than books, and visually representing information means sharing knowledge through more than just words, which is why these two areas were added when the English language arts standards were modified in 1996 by IRA and NCTE. Because societal expectations have changed, teaching students to communicate through words and sentences is no longer enough to prepare them to be literate contributors to society.

Although the topic of viewing and visually representing information is gaining attention, there is still a lot to be done. We must no longer think of literacy as "limited to what the tongue can articulate but what the mind can group" (Eisner, 2003, p. 342). According to Berghoff and Borgmann (2007), creating meaning requires much more than answering questions about a text or writing responses. Although comprehension is an important skill to develop, it must apply to more than the standard print media. To be productive citizens and active participants in the world, students must be able to view a variety of texts and understand what they are seeing. They must be able to visually represent their understanding through pictures, graphs, and other methods.

Comprehension still remains the common goal shared by viewing and visually representing nonprint media as well as reading and responding to printed text. However, to comprehend what they view, students need to use many reading skills that are associated with traditional text. Students must use metacognitive skills to monitor their viewing. As viewers, students must know whether they understand the material they are seeing and know what strategies must be used should they not comprehend the visual representation. Students must also view materials with a critical stance so that they are cognizant of the author's purpose. Instead of looking at individual aspects of what they view, students must look at the total picture. This is similar to reading printed text because we want students to read and not focus on each individual sound and word. Just as we don't seek to develop word callers with printed text, we don't want students to superficially state what is shown in something they view. We are asking students to explain their understanding and navigate diverse sign systems to demonstrate that knowledge.

There are many resources available to help teachers transform their classrooms into places where multiliteracies are valued. For instance, Anstey and Bull's (2006) *Teaching and Learning Multiliteracies: Changing Times, Changing Literacies* acknowledges that the printed text is not obsolete but rather just one type of text available. These authors' suggestions for classroom application can help educators change the way they teach literacy. We must value multiliteracies with even the youngest of children. In an article written by Crafton, Brennan, and Silvers (2007), we see a first-grade classroom where the teacher shares how her thinking of literacy is continually changing and how her young students thrive as they experience multiliteracies. Although many people may associate the term *multiliteracy* with the use of technology, multiliteracy entails much more (Caughlan, 2008). We are doing a disservice if we don't expose our students to a wide variety of visuals available. As Williams (2008) shares, the way we teach literacy today is not the way we learned it in the past, and is not the way it will be taught in the future.

To provide students with opportunities to view diverse media and show an understanding of mathematical material, we must provide a variety of experiences for this viewing, which might include plays, commercials, illustrations, graphs, and the Internet. Our classroom activities also require that students be able to visually represent what they are learning. Visually representing may be learned through dramatizations, charts, illustrations, advertisements, and other artistic creations. Just like any other type of communication, students must consider their purpose, the audience, and the form they are using when they visually represent information (Tompkins, 2009).

Students are often motivated to view and visually represent information while they are actively engaged in learning through the creation of new artifacts. Students realize the importance of these activities because they see these types of representations outside of the classroom. According to Kress (2003), students are often exposed to texts that are multimodal. Most students play video games, engage themselves on the Internet, and view images on the computer, on television, and in other media. Despite the fact that images are becoming the predominant form of text, the educational curriculum often remains focused on the traditional printed text (Williams, 2007).

By examining the literacy practices of adolescents, Moje, Overby, Tysvaer, and Morris (2008) find that students are engaged in a wide variety of literacy practices and texts every day. Students who may lack motivation with literacy activities completed within the school context may actively involve themselves in out-of-school literacies (Hinchman, Alvermann, Boyd, Brozo, & Vacca, 2004). Therefore, if we can connect literacies experienced within the school with literacies that students use on a daily basis outside of the school setting, we are helping them connect and see the importance of learning. We are providing authentic literacy activities that prepare students for the world in which they live.

This chapter begins with an overview of the benefits that can be gained by expanding our vision of literacy to include viewing and visually representing information. After that, specific classroom suggestions are shared for how we might turn our ideas into reality. Examples from a range of grade levels are included to help teachers see how other teachers incorporate viewing and visual representation in their math lessons. Along with developing word knowledge, students can learn to visually represent mathematical information and use dramatic representations to enhance their literacy skills while strengthening their mathematical knowledge.

Benefits of a Changing View of Literacy

Educators today must meet the needs of struggling readers, students whose primary language is different from the language of instruction, and students who may learn more easily through diverse modalities. We must also prepare students to respond to the continually changing literacy demands of the world around them. As we seek to meet the needs of an increasingly diverse group of students and strive to make our lessons more relevant to students' experiences outside the classroom, we see the rewards of our changing view of literacy. This literacy vision is not a set of activities or a prescribed list of skills, but rather a way of viewing our instruction to incorporate this vision throughout the day. Mathematics can provide a natural connection to viewing and visually representing information. Although teachers already use concrete objects and visuals to develop math skills, teachers can expand the use of viewing and visually representing throughout the mathematics curriculum so that more benefits are gained.

Emphasizes the Arts

Proponents of the arts should be pleased to see how highly valued the arts are within such a broad definition of literacy. Arts-based programs benefit other aspects of literacy, and research has shown a link between academic achievement in reading and an arts-based curriculum (Perkins, 1988). Instead of looking at the arts as an add-on or extra for the curriculum already taught in the classroom, the arts need to be integrated into students' learning in order for this type of literacy to develop.

Many researchers stress that students learn better and retain more if taught through diverse modalities (Eisner, 2003; Leland & Harste, 1994). Sarama and Clements (2003) have shown that very young students may learn faster if they have the opportunity to learn mathematics through songs, drawings, and building blocks. When we allow students to learn through these activities instead of marginalizing the arts, we make them part of the core curriculum (Eisner, 2003).

Supports Multiple Intelligences Theory and Transmediation

Gardner's (1985) multiple intelligences theory states there are eight intelligences: linguistic, logical-mathematical, musical, visual-spatial, bodily-kinesthetic, naturalistic, interpersonal, and intrapersonal. Many educators believe in Moran, Kornhaber, and Gardner's (2006) revised version of this theory, which adds a ninth intelligence, existential. This theory is not meant to limit students by categorizing them into specific types of learners but rather to broaden the way that educators present materials to students because what you do as an educator once you have a better understanding of students' strengths and weaknesses can play a major role in the learning process. Everyone can learn in multiple ways, and we all have strengths, weaknesses, and preferred styles of learning, all of which must be considered when planning instruction to support students' literacy development. In fact, Armstrong (1993) believes that we can use this information to appeal to individuals with learning disabilities by targeting their specific strengths.

The multiple intelligences theory encourages collaboration and allows students to work together to better meet their needs. Collaborating in flexible groups is a component of both the English language arts (IRA & NCTE, 1996) and NCTM (2000) standards. Students with strengths in one area can complement other students' strengths by working together to understand information presented in the classroom. This scaffolding helps students understand and learn more because of the students' zone of proximal development (Vygotsky, 1934/1978). Being productive members of society requires the use of several intelligences. By working together, students realize their own strengths and how to collaborate with others to develop diverse methods of learning. By providing rich experiences for students to interact directly with materials (Moran et al., 2006), teachers help students develop these intelligences.

The idea of providing students with a wide variety of experiences to support diverse learning ties into the theory of transmediation. Transmediation occurs when students take information they learned in one communication system (i.e., reading, writing, speaking, or listening) and show this information in another sign system (Leland & Harste, 1994). By creating visual representations based on the written word, they are doing just that. When students view something, such as a play or television commercial, then share their understanding through another sign system, they are experiencing transmediation. Moving between different systems of meaning allows for a deeper understanding of material (Short, Harste, & Burke, 1996). In our goal to help all students learn, we need to be sure that we are providing educational access to everyone. Students need to have the opportunity to learn and express themselves in a variety of communication systems.

This view of literacy may also be beneficial for those students who tend to struggle with the traditional form of literacy valued in schools (Hinchman et al., 2004). Students who have difficulty with reading printed texts may actually find that connecting with other types of literacy is beneficial (Flood & Lapp, 1995) and can then make intertextual connections between the diverse texts. Intertextuality, coined by Kristeva (1984), allows students to see that information they learned in a previous text can be applied to new knowledge. Therefore, seeing the link between visuals, printed words, and even oral language can strengthen literacy development. By looking at diverse media, students will realize that each of these media are not distinct resources, but rather that these types of text support various aspects of literacy and are interrelated. A diversity of texts can help students develop a more solid understanding of content knowledge.

Scaffolds English Learners

The idea of viewing and visually representing is beneficial for students whose first language may not be English. Research encourages educators to provide visuals when introducing new words to ELs. These visuals may be pictures, objects, or even actions (Helman & Burns, 2008). With visual representation, we ask students to show their knowledge through charts, posters, and even illustrations in class books they may be creating. ELs often learn more quickly when presented with such visuals, so the experience we provide them while viewing the creations and visually creating their own understanding can scaffold their learning.

In fact, research suggests that an arts-based curriculum may be especially beneficial for ELs (Spina, 2006). By encouraging ELs to create a visual or dramatize an action to go with a word, we help them expand their sight word vocabulary (Helman & Burns, 2008). Also, drama can allow them to better understand what they are learning because they are directly experiencing the lesson and developing a deeper understanding of the content. By providing multiple opportunities for students to read and experience words, we help students expand their vocabularies. Research shows that students must read words numerous times in order for the words to be learned (Hargis, Terhaar-Yonkers, Williams, & Reed, 1988), and a curriculum that includes viewing and visually representing material can provide even more opportunities for students to be exposed to words.

Our schools are becoming more and more culturally diverse. As our classrooms become more diverse, we must continue to strive to meet all students' needs. To prepare all learners for the world in which they live, we must use strategies that help students with diverse cultural backgrounds.

Enhances Out-of-School Literacies

As we continually strive to show our students connections between what they are learning in school and what they do outside of the classroom, fostering viewing and visual representation skills will help. These skills tie closely to the types of literacy our students use every day and the literacies with which they must become even more adept at understanding. When our students are not in school, they often spend countless hours engaging on the Internet, playing video games, and watching videos, movies, television shows, and commercials. Students are bombarded by all types of advertisements through other media (e.g., billboards, fliers). Although these visual representations are a common part of life, few students are savvy viewers. They need to be taught how to comprehend a variety of visual media to be truly literate.

Ties Easily to Technology

Technology is continually changing the world as we know it. Researchers and scholars warn us that if we don't allow students to navigate the wide variety of media that they encounter on a daily basis, including technology-enhanced media, we are doing a disservice to our students (McPherson,

2007). These are powerful literacies that are essential for preparing students to attain jobs and have an impact on the world (Finn, 1999). We must provide students with experiences to analyze various forms of media and be intelligent, knowledgeable consumers of it. If we are preparing students to be truly literate, they must understand technology and be able to comprehend, synthesize, and analyze all types of information and communication technologies.

When viewing information on the Internet, students select links that interest them. By doing this, students may develop a deeper understanding of some aspects of a particular topic but actually gain a more limited understanding of the overall topic. Also, students often look for visuals that explain the text on the Internet (Liu, 2005). Since research shows that 99% of U.S. public schools report that they have Internet access (National Center for Education Statistics, 2002), technology should be tied into the curriculum. Many researchers warn that technology should not be just an additional layer to the curriculum (Smolin & Lawless, 2003), but instead must be woven throughout the content. By using technology, students can access a variety of information and present information in a number of ways (Ikpeze & Boyd, 2007). In fact, all of the technologies to which students have access (e.g., Internet, e-mail, digital videos) are changing the way we see literacy and the knowledge that students will need to be successful in the workplace (Leu, 2000).

Encourages Struggling Readers

It is unsurprising that many activities pertaining to viewing and visually representing information involve drawing. Educators have shown that drawing can help modify the attitudes of students who may have negative attitudes toward writing and reading (Sneed, 1995). A wide variety of students are present in today's classroom, and they each come to us with different strengths. Some students' strength is drawing or visually representing, and allowing them to communicate in that manner can help improve their literacy skills and self-confidence (Sneed, 1995). Finally, drawing can help motivate learning-disabled students to develop other areas of literacy such as reading and writing (Sidelnick & Svoboda, 2000).

Turning Our Ideas Into Reality

Our goal as literacy leaders is to prepare students to be contributing members of society, and viewing and visually representing are two important aspects of literacy that need to be developed. Yet, it is not an easy task. Research shows that it is much easier to talk about a broadened definition of literacy than it is to actually apply it in the classroom (Sheridan-Thomas, 2007). The rest of this chapter is designed to provide a variety of easily implemented ideas for fostering viewing and visually representing mathematical information in the elementary classroom. Each of the activities discussed can nurture other aspects of literacy development such as talking and listening, but the ideas are presented here for teachers to see where viewing and visually representing information can tie into the classroom.

All of the activities discussed in the following sections fall into three categories. Some involve creating a visual representation on paper to reinforce students' mathematical word knowledge. Other activities use visual representation via drawing to help students communicate mathematical knowledge to others. Finally, the remaining activities are not visual in the traditional sense, but rather they involve students using their verbal and nonverbal skills to show mathematical meaning through drama.

The activities shared not only tie into the English language arts Standards 4 and 5, which focus on communicating knowledge appropriate for different purposes and audiences, but also help meet English language arts Standards 1, 6, 7, and 8, which specifically reference nonprint texts or technological resources (IRA & NCTE, 1996; see Appendix A). NCTM's (2000) process standards are also supported through viewing and visually representing information; students are expected not only to organize and communicate their mathematical thinking but also share their mathematical knowledge through representations (see Appendix B).

Reinforcing Word Knowledge Through Visual Representation

Helping students build their mathematical vocabulary is an important goal for any teacher. To do this, students need to develop a solid understanding of terms they encounter. While teachers should use concrete, hands-on experiences to help create this knowledge, viewing and visual representation activities can help reinforce that learning.

It is imperative that students develop an understanding of academic terms related to mathematics. Although some of these words are found solely within the field of mathematics, many may have multiple meanings and mean something very different in other contexts. By creating visuals and viewing these visual representations of content-specific vocabulary, students reinforce and expand their mathematical knowledge.

Each of the five strategies discussed in this section are designed to help students expand their mathematical vocabulary through the creation of visuals. The story problem visual isn't a concrete drawing but rather a visual that helps students understand how specific words can give clues to the operations they need to answer word problems. Creative concepts encourage students to use a variety of materials and ideas when helping others understand mathematical concepts. Lastly, picture dictionaries, multimeaning word cards, and the verbal-visual word association strategy involve drawing pictures and are designed to help students create items that build their vocabulary knowledge.

Conquering the Words in Word Problems. Many students struggle as they attempt to solve word problems, yet the terminology found in the problems is rarely unique. In fact, students see many of these words on a daily basis. In a word problem, a lot of information is expressed through a minimal number of words. Students must read the problem to determine which words provide key information for solving the problem. Students often have difficulty translating the words in the problem into the math symbols that represent the operations. For example, words as simple as *is* have a mathematical symbol—the equals sign—yet many students miss that tiny but important word in problems. A word problem visual can help students develop a better understanding of word usage within such problems. Even when students can complete mathematical equations, successfully completing word problems requiring the same operations is often difficult because students do not fully understand the operations needed to solve the problems.

One sixth-grade teacher created a visual to help students remember the order of operations and understand the vocabulary often seen in word problems. First, a paper was divided into five parts: the four corner areas plus a circle in the center. The four corner sections were numbered 1 through 4 counterclockwise, beginning in the top right corner, and the circle was numbered 5. The order in which the corner sections were numbered corresponds with the order the topics were learned in earlier grades: (1) addition, (2) subtraction, (3) multiplication, and (4) division. The concept of equality was placed in the center circle, position 5, because that concept is used with the other four processes. A large letter C can be drawn on the page to remind students to proceed counterclockwise around the four corner areas.

To complete the visual, the class was divided into small groups. Each group was then assigned the task of brainstorming a list of possible terms for one of the visual's five sections. One group had to think of words used for *plus*, one for *minus*, one for *times*, one for *divide by*, and another for *equals*. After the groups completed their assignment, each group orally shared their brainstormed creations on an overhead transparency. After each presentation, the rest of the class had the opportunity to share any additional ideas that might be added to that section. By the end of the activity, each student had created an individualized sheet with a variety of words on it. For example, Figure 5 is the sheet that Charles created.

Even though the visual is very basic, it helps students think about a variety of mathematical operations. The information is also arranged in such a way that it makes sense to students. They realize the order of operations and think about each operation in the order in which it was taught. By thinking about the words they see in word problems and talking about their ideas with peers, students can focus on the importance of specific words in word problems. Throughout the year, students continue to add words to the different sections as they talk with classmates and tackle more difficult mathematical word problems. This teacher found that many students continue to carry around their crumpled piece of paper containing the visual for years, and former students often mention how important that sheet of paper was for helping them decode word problems.

Creative Concepts. Often, the best way to develop a solid understanding of material is to teach it to others, and developing vocabulary knowledge is no exception. One idea is to have students select a concept they want to teach and develop a visual to reinforce the information. Students can work in small groups to brainstorm and share ways to visually depict the information. Students have to consider their audience and develop a unique way to help the audience retain the information. Through developing and

Figure 5. Visual Created by a Sixth Grader to Aid With Understanding Word Problems

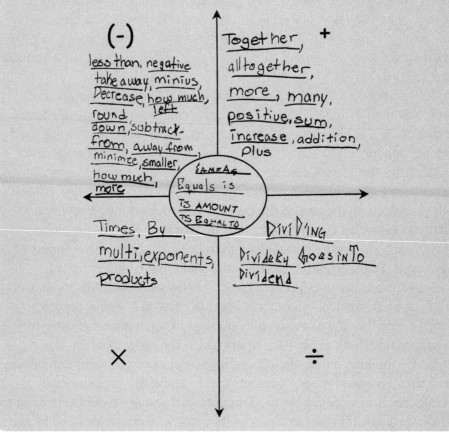

sharing their creation, students reinforce their own content knowledge. This strategy can work well with mathematical concepts at all grade levels in elementary school.

One teacher wanted sixth-grade students to develop creative ideas for representing the mathematical vocabulary they were learning. She presented them with the following scenario:

> You are now the teacher of a sixth-grade classroom. Your students are tired of looking up vocabulary words and writing their definitions. It is your job to find a creative way of representing a vocabulary word and its definition.

Then the students worked in groups of two or three to develop a visual to help their peers remember mathematical concepts. This activity not only provided the element of choice by allowing students to select a term but also gave them the opportunity to visually represent mathematical concepts. The opportunity to work together on these creations added even further to the educational value of the activity. As the students discussed ideas for their projects and brainstormed possible concepts, they used their oral language skills. Therefore, students not only refined their knowledge of the term they chose but also strengthened their understanding of a number of other mathematical concepts.

James and Beau decided to use their imagination and a number of paper clips to help their sixth-grade classmates understand the concept of gram. The visual the boys created shows that one paper clip is about one gram and includes the term's definition (see Figure 6). Their visual also includes groups of paper clips with approximate weights for each group.

Figure 6. Paper Clip Poster Created by Two Sixth Graders to Explain Grams

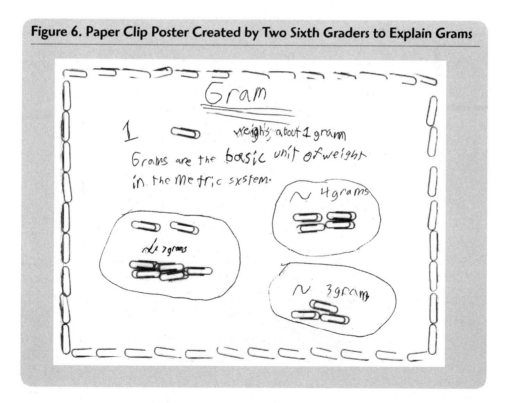

A group of three girls wanted to help their peers understand stem-and-leaf plots. Figure 7 shows the visual representation that the girls made to help others understand the concept. At the top of their brightly colored creation, they wrote a fact about stem-and-leaf plots, then added the definition and a sample below.

Both groups chose very different concepts and used different materials to make their creations. However, the entire class gained from this exercise. After the creations were developed, students orally shared their visuals with their peers. While listening to others in the class share their presentations,

Figure 7. Visual Created by Three Students to Teach Stem-and-Leaf Plots

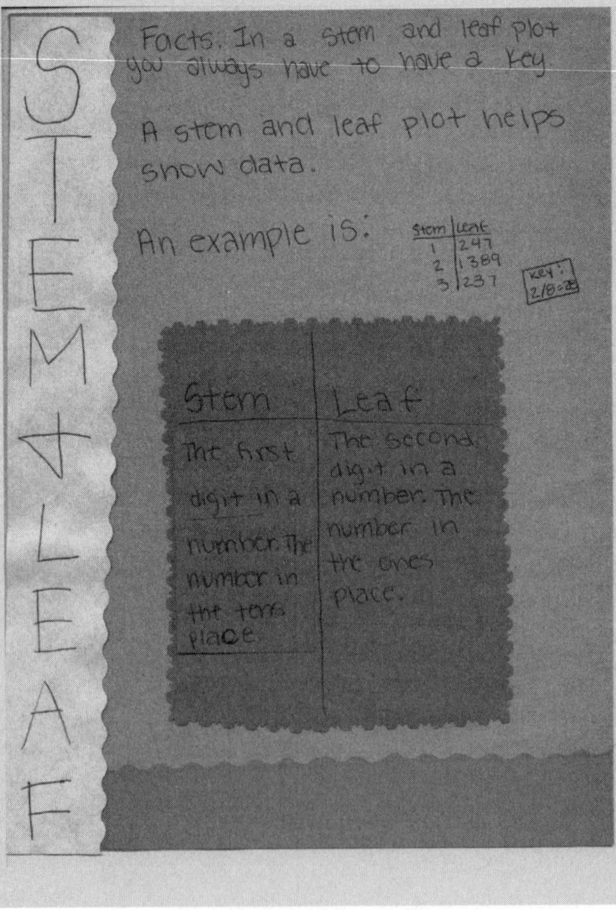

the students were able to synthesize new information on the concepts with knowledge that they already possessed. Students had the opportunity to view other presentations, talk about what they saw, and see how peers who chose the same concept may have represented it very differently. With the wide variety of mathematical concepts represented in this activity, the teacher chose to display these visuals in the classroom as a form of local text.

Picture Dictionaries. Dictionaries are often a wonderful source of information for students. When they are unsure of the meaning of a word, they may see a picture in a dictionary that helps them better understand the definition. Teachers sometimes use student-created picture dictionaries with ELs, since pictures have universal meaning. When the students create the images, they know what they are showing and can more easily remember the word's definition. I have seen many teachers of young students instruct them to add terms with which they are struggling to their picture dictionaries so that the visuals are individualized and meet the specific needs of each student.

One teacher had first graders create mathematical picture dictionaries. Although the text pages were alike for each student, there were blank areas for the students to individualize their dictionaries as needed. The students were enthusiastic about the project and eager to share how they visualized the concepts. The teacher chose concepts that the students had experienced with concrete objects previously in the classroom but were still having difficulty understanding. You could see the wheels spinning as the students thought about how to draw a picture to represent the concept of fewest. J.C. was excited when he came up with the idea to draw two groups of squares and circle the group with the fewest (see Figure 8). By drawing a picture and writing about the concept, J.C. reinforced previous learning. Later the teacher asked the students to color the pages before the sheets were cut and stapled to form a mathematical picture dictionary for the class to use as a local text.

Multimeaning Word Cards. In the elementary grades, students are taught to recognize and understand homophones and homonyms: Homophones are words that sound alike but are spelled differently, whereas homonyms not only sound alike but are also spelled the same. Teaching these terms is important because both types of words can include math concepts. There

Figure 8. Page From a First Grader's Math Picture Dictionary

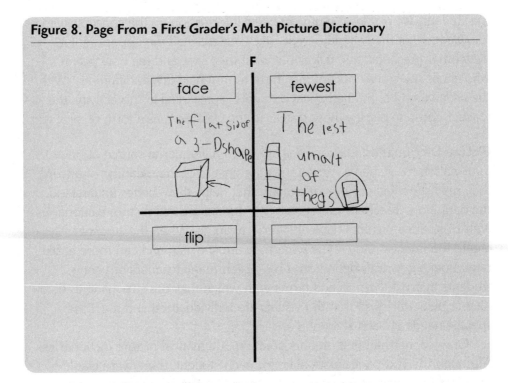

are many trade books that can be used to teach about these two types of words. Two popular books are Gwynne's (2005, 2006) *A Chocolate Moose for Dinner* and *The King Who Rained*. Also, teachers may enjoy Terban's (2007a, 2007b) *Eight Ate: A Feast of Homonym Riddles* and *How Much Can a Bare Bear Bear? What Are Homonyms and Homophones?*

It is important for students to learn that some of these words are actually mathematical terms. *Eight/ate* and *weight/wait* are just two of the homophones that students need to learn because one term in each set has a mathematical meaning. There are also homonyms with mathematical definitions, including *yard, mass,* and *volume*. Each of these words has a mathematical meaning plus a different meaning when used in other contexts. Although these words may cause some confusion for all students, homonyms can be particularly challenging for ELs.

As students are introduced to these words, teachers may have them create word cards of homonyms and homophones. On these multimeaning word cards, students can write the selected word and create an illustration to show the mathematical and everyday meanings of the word. If the term is a homophone, the teacher may choose to have students write both spellings for the word and draw a picture for each meaning. Then the students can share the cards with a partner or the teacher to ensure that the mathematical meaning is understood, which further reinforces the information. The thought processes required to discuss, write, and draw homonyms and homophones helps students understand that some words can have very different meanings, even though the words sound alike and sometimes are spelled the same.

For instance, one fourth-grade teacher used student-created word cards with Chloe, an EL who recently moved from South America to the United States. The teacher showed Chloe each word individually, and together they discussed the various meanings for each word. The teacher encouraged her to provide additional details for the words and wrote down what Chloe dictated. This provided an opportunity for the student to talk about some of the words. Then Chloe was given a set of cards with homophones or a homonym written on each. On each card, Chloe drew pictures of both meanings to help her remember that the words could have everyday meanings as well as meanings specific to math. On the cards, she also wrote several phrases and some of the details that she and her teacher had discussed.

On her multimeaning word card for the term *yard*, it is evident that Chloe is showing two different meanings for the term (see Figure 9). On the left-hand side of the card, Chloe illustrated and wrote about her yard at home. When she thinks of that definition of yard, she thinks about playing with a ball, her dog, and her dad. On the right-hand side of the card, we see how she might use the term in a mathematical setting. She showed herself with her hand at the top of her head as she is trying to measure herself with a yard stick. Chloe was eager to create and talk about the cards she created with her teacher, and the teacher felt that they helped Chloe understand a variety of homonyms and homophones.

Although the creation of multimeaning word cards has value, even more can be gained by actively incorporating them into the classroom as a form of local text. If the student-created cards are made on large sheets of paper, they can easily become part of a word wall in the classroom. Word walls often contain content area vocabulary that students might find difficult. The cards can even be photocopied and made into a matching

Figure 9. A Fourth-Grade EL's Multimeaning Word Card

game for students who need the additional reinforcement to work with during their free time.

Verbal-Visual Word Association Strategy. This strategy was designed many years ago to provide an alternative to rote memorization of vocabulary definitions (Eeds & Cockrum, 1985). Later, the strategy was modified and a visual aid added (Readence, Bean, & Baldwin, 1998). Researchers have implemented the verbal-visual word association strategy into classrooms and found support for diverse learners (Hopkins & Bean, 1999). This vocabulary strategy can easily be tied into a number of content areas including mathematics.

To successfully complete this activity, the student divides a piece of paper into four sections. In one of the four sections, the student writes the term or concept. Then in another section, the student draws an illustration to help remember the meaning of the term. Not only is the drawing important as a memory tool but also as a visual representation of the student's personal association with the term. Thus, remembering the term is now more than just rote memorization of content vocabulary. In a third section, the student writes the term's definition. Finally, the student uses the term in a sentence in the last section.

A second-grade student, Sherrell, created a verbal-visual word association for the term *estimate*, which is shown in Figure 10. In the first section, she listed the vocabulary term *estimate*. She also explained what *estimate* means to her, emulating something her teacher has probably said often in class, "Make your best guess." Throughout the year, Sherrell's teacher filled a jar with different items and allowed students to estimate the number of items the jar contained. When it came to drawing a visual, Sherrell thought about a jar of marbles that she had seen in class and drew a simple illustration of that jar. To complete the activity, she reflected back on an activity for which the class had to estimate the number of marbles in the jar and wrote a sentence about that experience using the term *estimate*.

Sometimes with very young students, teachers create the image used in the verbal-visual word association activity. However, those drawings are less meaningful to the students because they do not represent the students' personal connections to the term. By having the students draw something

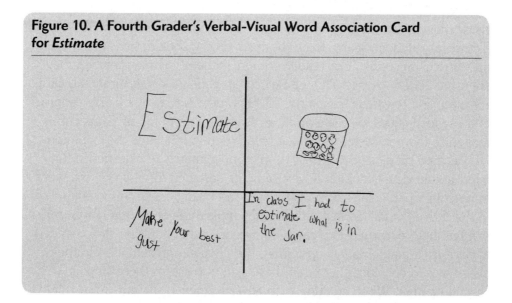

Figure 10. A Fourth Grader's Verbal-Visual Word Association Card for *Estimate*

that they associate with the term and come up with a sentence using the word, they are much more apt to remember the concept later.

When I use this strategy with very young students, I sometimes modify the four sections of the paper so that they are not equal in size. I find that students need much less room to write the term than they do to complete the rest of the activity. Therefore, I allow only a small amount of space for the students to write the actual vocabulary word and create larger boxes for each of the other three parts of the activity. One sheet of paper can be large enough to complete the activity for four vocabulary words.

Visually Communicating Information

Along with reinforcing word knowledge through visual representation, students can also use it to communicate mathematical information. Instead of focusing on specific terms, the students visually explain broader topics. These visuals may share how to perform certain mathematical operations, provide information that enhances oral reports, or even help convey the meaning of student-created story problems. The important thing to remember is that the use of the visuals allows students to develop their viewing and visual representation skills.

Persuasive Advertisements. An excellent time to discuss propaganda techniques and the ability to influence other people's decisions through visual representations is when students learn about persuasive writing. Elementary students learn about these six propaganda devices as part of the curriculum so they can readily recognize these techniques when they are used: glittering generality, name calling, bandwagon, testimonial, card stacking, and rewards (Tompkins, 2009). Students may enjoy using some of these techniques to create an advertisement to see if their peers can recognize the persuasive technique being used to influence their opinions.

Because many students have ample opportunities to experience the Internet and view television advertisements designed to persuade the viewer to react in a particular manner, students can readily relate this activity to the outside world. In this activity, they must think about mathematical content they've learned to create an advertisement about the steps needed to perform a mathematical operation, then make a presentation to their classmates to convince them that they need to perform these steps in a certain manner. When creating such advertisements, students must think about the purpose of the visual and the audience with whom they are trying to communicate.

One fourth-grade teacher decided to have her students complete this activity when her students were learning about propaganda techniques. The teacher began by looking up the definition with the class, then gave a few examples of these techniques. The students discussed the media, television, and advertisements and were surprised to learn that advertising is designed to persuade them. They had never really thought about advertising or its purpose.

The class then discussed the purpose of advertisements and targeting audiences. The teacher introduced the idea that most persuasive advertisements use a catchy slogan to help convince people and make their point memorable. Students were quick to recognize and share slogans they heard on television, such as McDonald's "i'm lovin' it ™" and Nike's "Just Do It. ™" This led to a discussion about the people students saw in those commercials and the implied message that "everyone is doing it, so you should, too."

Each student evaluated his or her favorite multiplying method and created a persuasive advertisement to convince classmates to use that method. Borrowing from the media reviewed, many students even came up with slogans. In Figure 11A, the student encourages peers to "Do it the Lattice Way Not the baddest way!" According to the visual, the method is described as quick and fun. Also, the directions are listed to instruct readers on the method's steps. The student wants the audience to see value in the lattice method.

Another student decided to compare the way people read math problems to the way they read written words on a page. As shown in Figure 11B, she wrote at the top of her visual, "You May Read Left-to-Right, but in Multiplying Work Right-to-Left! (2 digit by 2 digit)."

All of the students presented their advertisements to the class, and then the entire class voted on which student had the most convincing advertisement. This activity not only drew on visual communication but also required students to articulate their thoughts to their peers. Teachers may even incorporate technology into the activity by recording the presentations or sharing photographs of them with others via the Internet.

Although these examples were created by fourth graders, this activity can be modified for younger students. Primary-grade students can talk

Figure 11. Two Persuasive Advertisements by Fourth Graders

A

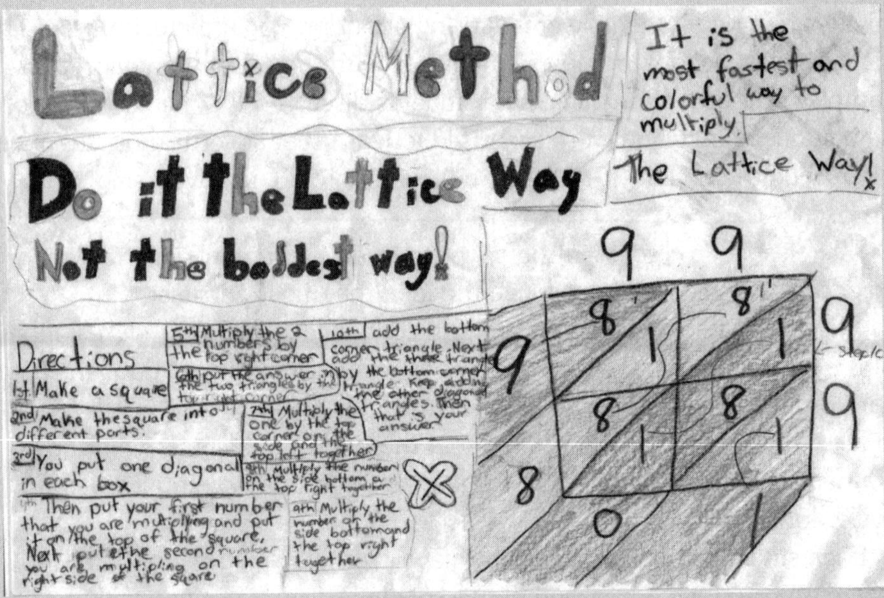

B

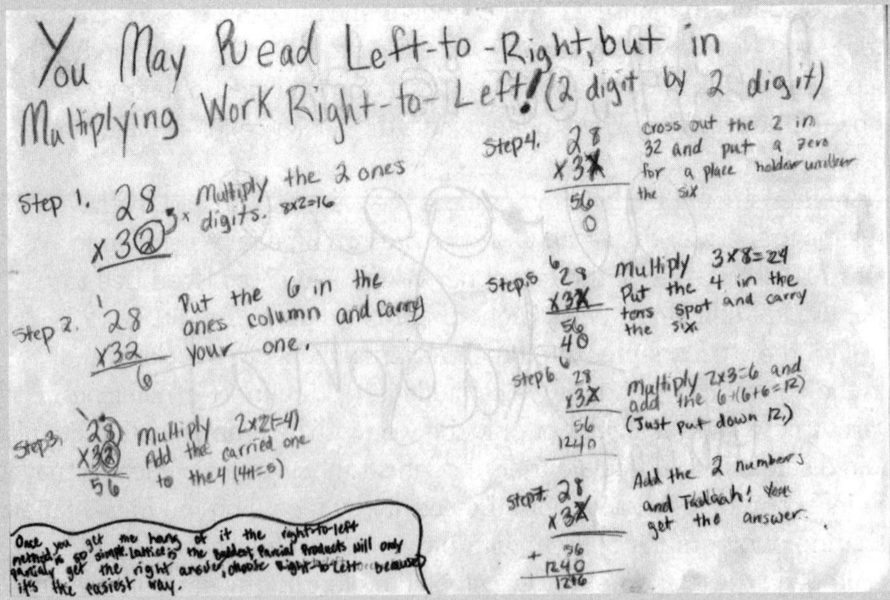

about some of the commercials they see on television and discuss the ways that advertisements try to persuade people to buy a product, see a movie, or even visit an amusement park. The teacher can list those suggestions on the board, then focus on what the students have learned in mathematics. Why is it important to use concrete objects when you are learning to add? Why should students subtract or add columns in math problems from right to left? Why should students learn to create and read bar graphs?

After discussing these topics as a class, students can work in groups and choose a persuasion strategy to create an advertisement encouraging others to use concrete objects or complete mathematical problems in a certain manner. Then the students can share their advertisements with another class. Even though your students might not know the specific term for the propaganda device used, creating an advertisement is an excellent way to introduce the concept of propaganda and another way to incorporate viewing and visually representing into the younger grades.

Class-Created Mathematical Trade Books. For class-created books, each student contributes a page, then the book is laminated and used in classroom libraries or checked out by individual students to share at home. The activity has a great deal of value. Along with developing writing skills, students feel pride in the fact that they are authors. They are motivated to do their best writing for this project and eager to read the class-created book. Creating mathematical trade books with students can have additional benefits by reinforcing the mathematical skills and providing a literacy–mathematics connection. Students might share these books with younger students or even peers.

In one fourth-grade class, the teacher read the mathematical trade book *Each Orange Had 8 Slices: A Counting Book* (Giganti, 1999). This is a wonderful book for learning about patterns, multiplying, and solving math problems. Along with the engaging text, students are exposed to bright, colorful pictures that complement the math problems. As the fourth-grade teacher read the story to the students, she introduced multiplication properties (e.g., communicative, associative, zero), and the class discussed each of the properties and why they are important. While answering the questions presented on each page, the students noticed the repetitive phrase that starts each page, "On my way...." The class discussed the qualities that made the story enjoyable. Students mentioned that they liked the pictures and that each page had a puzzle to solve. As the students more closely analyzed the text, they noticed that each puzzle was created from three sets of numbers and that there were three questions to go along with each puzzle. It made math fun.

The class then decided to create their own trade book that was laminated and saved, so they could reread the pages later and try to solve their peers' math problems. This class-created book, *On the Way, a Fourth Grader Saw...Can You Solve Equation?*, was modeled after the children's book they had just read. Because the students each created a page for this local text, they had to think about how to make a good puzzle. The illustration had to be accurate and complement the text on the page. Also, the students needed to be sure that the text made sense and that there was a solution.

J.T.'s page for the class book relates to buying ice cream (see Figure 12). His statements are clear, and it is easy to understand the problem. J.T. actually wrote a pretty tricky mathematical problem, though, whether he meant to or not. After reading the first three lines of the page, one expects to be asked for the total number of scoops, but the final question doesn't ask that. Pages like the one J.T. created require the reader to read the problem carefully.

The picture J.T. drew accurately represents his math problem. The type of illustrations found in a class-created book might be very different from drawings students make for themselves to help them figure out simple word problems. Crespo and Kyriakides (2007) conducted research with first-through fourth-grade students and found that two types of drawing—iconic and pictographic—are often created by students in math classrooms. Iconic drawings are very basic. Instead of creating detailed, visually appealing drawings, students might draw four circles with a line through the middle of them to illustrate a problem such as the following:

> Mary has four Reuben sandwiches. She is walking to school and finds that seven of her friends forgot to pack their lunch. How can she divide the four sandwiches so that each of her friends has something to eat?

However, to create a pictographic drawing, the student might draw a girl at school with her seven friends who forgot to pack their lunches. This picture would be much more detailed and more closely resemble pictures that students often see in mathematical trade books.

Figure 12. A Fourth Grader's Contribution to a Class-Created Mathematical Trade Book

On my way to get ice cream I saw 3 boys.

Each boy had 1 Ice cream cone.
Each cone had 2 scoops.
How many Scoops of Ice cream did each Boy have?

Crespo and Kyriakides (2007) stress that we can use the pictures that students create when solving math problems as "windows into their mathematical thinking" (p. 122). Regardless of the type of drawing produced, we can gain much more insight by talking about these drawings. A student can be asked to share why he or she did or did not include certain information in the illustration and which parts of the picture help the reader solve the problem. Did the student draw the illustration as they were writing the problem or reading another mathematical problem, or was the drawing created afterward? Would it be helpful if the illustration were more or less detailed? Was the amount of detail related to the purpose of the illustration? If the student created the visual to help solve a math problem, was the picture different from the type of visual he or she would make to go with a math problem created for a trade book that others might read? Why or why not? Did the students take into consideration the audience for the visual when creating it? These types of conversations can help students gain even more from drawings they create through mathematical lessons. As with other types of literacy, students are required to think about the audience for the drawing and the purpose behind creating the visual.

After the class book was made, the students read through the book and attempted to solve the problems. Before making the text a permanent part of the classroom, the fourth graders shared their creation with first-grade partners. A local text such as a class-made book shared with other grade levels has a lot of value in the classroom.

Oral Report Visuals. Oral reports can serve a valuable purpose in the classroom by helping students learn to research, organize, and communicate information to an audience. Along with oral and written communication skills, the visuals students create for oral presentations can help promote viewing and visual representation. Oral reports are an excellent activity that teachers can use to tie literacy skills into any content area, and math is no exception.

The possibilities for topics that tie into mathematics are practically endless. Students might be asked to research and report on the epistemology, or word origins, of some interesting mathematical terms. The students may study and share information on currencies used in other parts of the world or research and collect data on lunches purchased in the cafeteria to determine which ones are the most popular. Students may even search the Internet to determine the cost to eat at a number of restaurants with online menus and then graph the results to share with others. Another idea is for students to interview people of a variety of ages to see how the teaching of math has changed over time and present their results to their classmates. Also, students might research a famous mathematician and share what the world gained from that person. Selecting a topic is only the first of these seven steps, which are encouraged when creating a mathematical oral report:

1. *Select a topic.* The element of choice is important here. The class might brainstorm a few ideas and then each student can select a topic from the options. By allowing the class to select their topics, students feel that they are part of the decision-making process and are motivated to do a good job.

2. *Obtain information.* This can be done through a variety of methods. Students might conduct interviews, go online to research information, read books, or use any combination of these ideas. The important thing is for students to use factual mathematical information as part of their presentations.

3. *Take notes.* Students must write down information that they think they might want to share in the report.

4. *Compile and organize information.* At this time, students decide what is important and put this information on note cards. It is important that they learn to use keywords and not write down everything they plan to say.

5. *Create visual aids.* Students have to determine what information can be easily shared through a visual aid. There are many types of visual aids that students can use, including environmental print, graphs, charts, videos, and concrete objects. The visual aids should enhance the presentation and not take the place of or be redundant with the information presented in the oral report. The ability to create an effective visual aid is a difficult skill to learn. Students have to decide what information is better shared through words in the oral report and what can be shared better through the visual medium.

6. *Organize the report.* Students should make sure that their reports make sense. They must pick the order in which their note cards will be shared so that their information is easily understood and determine the order in which they want to share the visual images they created. Practicing the oral report at this step helps students do their best possible job.

7. *Present the report.* Even though this is the last step, it isn't the most important one. All of the steps are important. Again, choice can help make oral reports more fun for the student. The class might brainstorm some interesting ways to present their information. Teachers may find that the oral reports are better prepared as a small group the first time the class creates them. In addition, the students have the added benefit of collaborative learning.

A fourth- through sixth-grade teacher at a Montessori school decided to have her students develop group oral reports that would incorporate viewing and visual representation as well as mathematical skills. The teacher began by having the students brainstorm topics they could research for their oral reports. The following are some of the ideas the class came up with:

- Money around the world
- Graphing favorite foods, math symbols, colors, and animals of the entire school
- War strategies that use math
- How money has changed over the years (e.g., inflation)
- Famous mathematicians
- A study of how different math tools (e.g., compass) were created
- Architecture

The students had several guidelines to follow. Each group's oral report was to last three to five minutes, a visual aid had to be used, and each student in the group had to speak during the presentation. The students chose their own groups and then selected their topics.

Most of the class chose to research favorite foods, animals, and colors in the school. The students were aware that these are not topics specifically related to mathematics, so they had to create visuals (i.e., time lines, charts, diagrams) that incorporated mathematical skills. As part of this project, students had the opportunity to practice their oral language skills by asking questions of peers in each of the classrooms at the school, listening to responses, and talking about the process. The groups also created graphs and other visuals to illustrate their findings.

One group of boys, B.J., Harrison, and Ely, decided to research war strategies because war was an area of interest that began when the class talked about Veterans Day. However, when the boys started researching the topic, they decided to look at the casualties of each U.S. war to compare the number of casualties in a graph. Therefore, the three boys were able to research an area of interest to them, develop their literacy skills, and enhance their mathematical knowledge through the visual. The graph they created to mount on their poster showed the number of casualties in eight wars beginning with the Revolutionary War and ending with the War on Terrorism. The boys found the information and the pictures for their poster on the Internet. The pictures included the famous photograph of soldiers raising the flag on Iwo Jima and the advertisement for Rosie the Riveter saying, "We can do it!" During their oral report, the boys explained the differences between the wars and what caused more or less deaths in each. The group also created visuals to help share the information and statistics with their viewers.

This oral report was presented as a skit, so each of the three boys could talk and add to the report. The boys typed up their presentation as follows:

Harrison: As you can see the casualties for the wars shoot up in WW2 when it shot up to 77,000,000 and in the civil war it was pretty high to.

B.J.: YEAH I KNOW!

Harrison: yep it's pretty big huh?

Ely: was the battle of Iwo Jima a bloody battle because I saw a picture and it was pretty cool.

B.J.: yeah and then the photo where the united states were putting up the flag in Iwo Jima they didn't take the picture in the heat of battle they took while the people where posing

Ely: the person on the picture that said we can do it her name was Rosie the riveter in WW2 they made a drug called penicillin it fought germs that infected wounds.

Harrison: that is the WW2 part of our oral report now for the Vietnam in the Vietnam war they had much faster and much more high tech planes than in WW2 therefore less deaths in the air force but there was also less deaths than in the WW2 because there were a lot more germ fighting drugs so when they got wounded they could help and clean the wounded.

B.J.: the terrorism is still going on now and that is a very bloody battle.

Ely: when we were in the WW2 Hitler's army was very big and he thought he would rule the world.

Harrison: so did I!

Through these reports, the students gained valuable research skills and had the opportunity to view and scrutinize information on the Internet and in other texts. Then the students determined the information they needed to write their reports and selected the best methods to visually represent their topics. Peers had an opportunity to view the information during the oral reports and ask questions of the presenters. Mathematical knowledge was reinforced through the creation of a variety of charts, including pie graphs and bar charts. Afterward, the students were able to reflect on how they might better take the audience into consideration when representing information. Along with all of these important skills, the students had an opportunity to see how math ties into the world.

Dramatic Representations

Along with creating concrete visuals that students can view, there are many benefits to incorporating dramatic representations into the classroom. Research has shown that even the act of creating visualizations in students' minds helps with their understanding of topics (Ross & Roe, 1977). Furthermore, drama helps motivate students and interest them in the material. Drama naturally motivates students to learn because they are actively engaged in the activity and eager to complete the experience. Also, research has shown that drama has the potential to influence attitudes on learning (DeRita & Weaver, 1991). Therefore, very young students who are developing attitudes and interests may develop positive attitudes toward mathematics when they experience a connection between drama and math.

According to McMaster (1998), drama is a form of communication that is meaningful to students and allows them to develop skills through social interaction. Drama encourages collaboration among students as they work together to act out a concept. Teachers benefit from the use of drama in the classroom because the dramatic presentations provide immediate feedback on whether students understand the concepts (McMaster, 1998).

Through dramatic activities, students must be aware of their audience. They not only articulate their ideas through words but also convey their thoughts through actions. This type of acting helps provide experiences for students who learn best through bodily-kinesthetic activities (Gardner, 1987).

Informal Drama Activities. Allowing students to view dramatic activities and visually represent meaning through verbal and nonverbal dramatizations is an excellent activity for promoting literacy development. Although plays require a significant amount of work and time from the teacher and the students, many of the same benefits with less time and work can be achieved through informal drama. As students are involved in the dramatic experience, they develop a deeper understanding of terms. The audience members must observe the drama, listen closely, and think about what is happening to comprehend the presentation. The students evaluate the activity by determining whether it makes sense and may think about other ways to demonstrate the same concepts. Although McMaster (1998) shares a number of literacy benefits that can be achieved by incorporating drama into classroom lessons, many basic mathematical concepts can be reinforced through informal dramatic activities. Also, drama can broaden vocabulary knowledge (Duffelmeyer & Duffelmeyer, 1979).

For example, one kindergarten teacher uses this type of activity to help students demonstrate their understanding of the mathematical concept of positional words such as *over*, *under*, *beside*, and *on*. Helping students understand and use positional words is a common concept in the kindergarten mathematics curriculum and is listed in many kindergarten textbooks and curriculum guides. As the class sits on the carpet in the room, the teacher reads the Big Book *The Napping House* (Wood, 1991). This repetitive tale appeals to young students with its illustrations and cumulative rhyme. As the teacher carefully reviews each page, the students show the position of each character (granny, flea, mouse, cat, dog, and boy) with individual stick puppets they've created for each.

Students are given the opportunity to look at a page and then say something they notice about the page using the positional words. During experiences like this, students might say something such as, "The mouse is beside the cat." Then each of the students arrange the mouse and cat puppets to show that sentence. Furthermore, the students use positional vocabulary to discuss changes that occur in the illustrations. For example, on one page granny is *beside* the boy instead of *on* the boy. Students then talk about how the position of granny has changed by using the positional words.

This type of learning helps students understand mathematical concepts and reinforces learning because the lesson encourages the use of physical movement. Later the students will remember the meaning because they were actively involved in experiencing the words. Teachers might use other activities involving bodily-kinesthetic responses to help students experience and act out other mathematical terms, such as *dividing*, *adding*, and *subtracting*. Although concrete objects and manipulatives are essential materials for learning mathematics, informal drama activities offer the teacher another opportunity to improve literacy skills and expand mathematical understanding.

Besides younger students, who enjoy and learn from these types of informal drama activities, older students who struggle with basic concepts may benefit from the reinforcement provided through the drama also. ELs may expand their vocabulary through hearing the words or mathematical terms and participating in the activities.

Mathematical Story Dramatizations. Students benefit from acting out teacher-created mathematical stories. Armstrong (1994) created a story to teach first graders about time, and as he shared his story with the students, they acted it out. This type of dramatic activity can be tied to mathematical trade books easily. Students aren't required to create elaborate costumes or a backdrop for this type of activity; they need only portray the characters and act out the mathematical story. These story dramatizations are more formal than the previously discussed drama activities. Often a greater amount of time is put into preparing this activity or writing the script, and there is an audience for the presentation. Students consider the audience when they act out their part and realize through their voice, movements, or facial expressions—depending on the type of presentation—that they are communicating mathematical information with others.

A third-grade teacher created a short play, *The Story of Place Value!*, to reinforce concepts that the students were learning. In the play, there is a very confused king. Although he rules a land that is rich and fertile for growing amazing candy, the people of the land have to pay taxes in the form of rice. The people love what the king grows, and therefore he receives many bags of rice. However, he cannot figure out how to count the bags because he only has 10 fingers. The king then asks each of his three bright sons to suggest a solution. One son finally comes to the conclusion that, if the rice bags are grouped in piles of 10, the bags can be counted more easily. The king is very happy and gives his crown to the son who came up with the answer.

The students loved performing and viewing the play. This activity served to help the students understand the mathematical concept of place value. As an extension activity and to build on the students' enthusiasm, the third-graders created their own plays, which incorporated mathematical concepts. The students performed their plays for their peers and were able to demonstrate reading, writing, listening, and talking skills. The students learned to visually represent and view mathematical concepts that were presented in a nonprint format.

The power of drama cannot be underestimated. Although many teachers may hesitate to include it in the curriculum, drama can be a very educational activity at any age level and a means to encourage literacy skill development while connecting learning to mathematics. Once again, teachers need to make sure that the time involved is justified by the learning that is occurring. There is little benefit from spending a great deal of class time creating costumes and scenery when a simple and easily made item can serve to let the viewers know which student is which character. In the student-created play previously discussed, a paper crown represented the king. Students could wear tags around their necks stating their characters' names, too.

If teachers do not want to be concerned with movement on stage or simple items for costumes, the class may present their plays as Readers Theatre. Scripts for Readers Theatre can be found in books, located on the Internet, or created by the students and teacher. Those created by the class have additional literacy benefits because students also develop their written language skills.

Students can sit or stand as they read their parts, since there is no movement or costumes to help students portray their characters. Thus, students are required to depict their characters through vocal tone, inflection, and juncture. By using Readers Theatre for drama, the focus is on oral language skills and not on the ability to visually represent characters through costume and movement. Students need to use prosody to express the feelings and beliefs of their characters. Readers Theatre has also been shown to benefit struggling readers (Rinehart, 1999; Tyler & Chard, 2000), and the benefits of incorporating drama into the classroom can far outweigh the time spent on the activity.

WHERE DO I GO FROM HERE?

As educators, we must be prepared to support a broad view of literacy including viewing and visually representing. Harste, Woodward, and Burke (1984) encourage us to allow students to generate and share their ideas through dancing, drawing, and dramatic activities. Students at all levels need the opportunity to interact and experience a range of media and texts. Just as visual literacies are becoming more prevalent in our lives, visual literacy is one more way to reach our students. Students must see that we can view more than just a "text-centric approach" (Piro, 2002, p. 127). No longer solely found in books or other printed matter, valued texts may sometimes be read in a nonlinear manner.

We can integrate the arts more easily by collaborating with colleagues in other areas of the curriculum (Berghoff, Borgmann, & Parr, 2005). This type of teaching helps us incorporate the newest aspect of language arts—viewing and visually representing—into areas such as mathematics. Through activities such as those discussed in this chapter, we can continue to foster literacy development and help students develop a deeper understanding of mathematical concepts.

IRA/NCTE Standards for the English Language Arts

The vision guiding these standards is that all students must have the opportunities and resources to develop the language skills they need to pursue life's goals and to participate fully as informed, productive members of society. These standards assume that literacy growth begins before children enter school as they experience and experiment with literacy activities—reading and writing, and associating spoken words with their graphic representations. Recognizing this fact, these standards encourage the development of curriculum and instruction that make productive use of the emerging literacy abilities that children bring to school. Furthermore, the standards provide ample room for the innovation and creativity essential to teaching and learning. They are not prescriptions for particular curriculum or instruction.

Although we present these standards as a list, we want to emphasize that they are not distinct and separable; they are, in fact, interrelated and should be considered as a whole.

1. Students read a wide range of print and nonprint texts to build an understanding of texts, of themselves, and of the cultures of the United States and the world; to acquire new information; to respond to the needs and demands of society and the workplace; and for personal fulfillment. Among these texts are fiction and nonfiction, classic and contemporary works.

2. Students read a wide range of literature from many periods in many genres to build an understanding of the many dimensions (e.g., philosophical, ethical, aesthetic) of human experience.

3. Students apply a wide range of strategies to comprehend, interpret, evaluate, and appreciate texts. They draw on their prior experience, their interactions with other readers and writers, their knowledge

From International Reading Association & National Council of Teachers of English. (1996). *Standards for the English Language Arts*. Newark, DE; Urbana, IL: Authors. Reprinted with permission.

of word meaning and of other texts, their word identification strategies, and their understanding of textual features (e.g., sound-letter correspondence, sentence structure, context, graphics).

4. Students adjust their use of spoken, written, and visual language (e.g., conventions, style, vocabulary) to communicate effectively with a variety of audiences and for different purposes.

5. Students employ a wide range of strategies as they write and use different writing process elements appropriately to communicate with different audiences for a variety of purposes.

6. Students apply knowledge of language structure, language conventions (e.g., spelling and punctuation), media techniques, figurative language, and genre to create, critique, and discuss print and nonprint texts.

7. Students conduct research on issues and interests by generating ideas and questions, and by posing problems. They gather, evaluate, and synthesize data from a variety of sources (e.g., print and nonprint texts, artifacts, people) to communicate their discoveries in ways that suit their purpose and audience.

8. Students use a variety of technological and information resources (e.g., libraries, databases, computer networks, video) to gather and synthesize information and to create and communicate knowledge.

9. Students develop an understanding of and respect for diversity in language use, patterns, and dialects across cultures, ethnic groups, geographic regions, and social roles.

10. Students whose first language is not English make use of their first language to develop competency in the English language arts and to develop understanding of content across the curriculum.

11. Students participate as knowledgeable, reflective, creative, and critical members of a variety of literacy communities.

12. Students use spoken, written, and visual language to accomplish their own purposes (e.g., for learning, enjoyment, persuasion, and the exchange of information).

NCTM Standards for Mathematics

Content Standards

. . . .

Number and Operations

Instructional programs from prekindergarten through grade 12 should enable all students to—

- Understand numbers, ways of representing numbers, relationships among numbers, and number systems
- Understand meanings of operations and how they relate to one another
- Compute fluently and make reasonable estimates

Algebra

Instructional programs from prekindergarten through grade 12 should enable all students to—

- Understand patterns, relations, and functions
- Represent and analyze mathematical situations and structures using algebraic symbols
- Use mathematical models to represent and understand quantitative relationships
- Analyze change in various contexts

Geometry

Instructional programs from prekindergarten through grade 12 should enable all students to—

- Analyze characteristics and properties of two- and three-dimensional geometric shapes and develop mathematical arguments about geometric relationships
- Specify locations and describe spatial relationships using coordinate geometry and other representational systems
- Apply transformations and use symmetry to analyze mathematical situations
- Use visualization, spatial reasoning, and geometric modeling to solve problems

Measurement

Instructional programs from prekindergarten through grade 12 should enable all students to—

- Understand measurable attributes of objects and the units, systems, and processes of measurement
- Apply appropriate techniques, tools, and formulas to determine measurements

Data Analysis and Probability

Instructional programs from prekindergarten through grade 12 should enable all students to—

- Formulate questions that can be addressed with data and collect, organize, and display relevant data to answer them
- Select and use appropriate statistical methods to analyze data
- Develop and evaluate inferences and predictions that are based on data
- Understand and apply basic concepts of probability

Process Standards

Problem Solving

Instructional programs from prekindergarten through grade 12 should enable all students to—

- Build new mathematical knowledge through problem solving
- Solve problems that arise in mathematics and in other contexts
- Apply and adapt a variety of appropriate strategies to solve problems
- Monitor and reflect on the process of mathematical problem solving

Reasoning and Proof

Instructional programs from prekindergarten through grade 12 should enable all students to—

- Recognize reasoning and proof as fundamental aspects of mathematics
- Make and investigate mathematical conjectures
- Develop and evaluate mathematical arguments and proofs
- Select and use various types of reasoning and methods of proof

Communication

Instructional programs from prekindergarten through grade 12 should enable all students to—

- Organize and consolidate their mathematical thinking through communication
- Communicate their mathematical thinking coherently and clearly to peers, teachers, and others
- Analyze and evaluate the mathematical thinking and strategies of others
- Use the language of mathematics to express mathematical ideas precisely

Connections

Instructional programs from prekindergarten through grade 12 should enable all students to—

- Recognize and use connections among mathematical ideas
- Understand how mathematical ideas interconnect and build on one another to produce a coherent whole

• Recognize and apply mathematics in contexts outside of mathematics

Representation

Instructional programs from prekindergarten through grade 12 should enable all students to—

- Create and use representations to organize, record, and communicate mathematical ideas
- Select, apply, and translate among mathematical representations to solve problems
- Use representations to model and interpret physical, social, and mathematical phenomena

An Annotated Bibliography of Recently Published Mathematical Trade Books

Adler, D.A. (2006). *You Can, Toucan, Math: Word Problem-Solving Fun.* New York: Holiday House.

> Through the pages of this book, the reader will have the opportunity to solve 21 simple math word problems using addition, subtraction, multiplication, and division. Each word problem is about a different type of bird. For each word problem, the author explains the various ways the reader might find the answer. Other books by the author pertaining to shapes, height, and distance may be of interest.

Ball, J. (2005). *Go Figure: A Totally Cool Book About Numbers.* New York: Dorling Kindersley.

> This is a book that teachers might use as a resource. The text isn't meant to be read from front to back in a linear fashion, but it is a great book for finding interesting information to share with students. In addition, students might want to peruse the pages. The book shows that math is important and is all around us. The text is full of brainteasers, magic tricks, puzzles, and scissor-and-paper activities.

Burns, M. (2008). *Spaghetti and Meatballs for All! A Mathematical Story.* New York: Scholastic.

> The focus of this book is on developing an understanding of area and perimeter. A variety of ethnicities are represented within the pages, and gender roles are reversed by having Mr. Comfort do the cooking. A wonderful dinner is planned, but when the guests arrive, things get confusing. As tables are moved together, there are fewer places at the table for people to eat. The number of chairs is the same, but something is wrong. This book includes ideas for adults who are helping children understand perimeter and area.

Calvert, P. (2006). *Multiplying Menace: The Revenge of Rumpelstiltskin.* Watertown, MA: Charlesbridge.

This book may appeal more to readers who know the tale of Rumpelstiltskin. In this book, Rumpelstiltskin seeks payment from the queen for gold that he spun. He makes various threats to the kingdom if the queen doesn't pay, but would be satisfied with having the queen's young son work off the debt. This book deals with multiplying whole numbers and multiplying fractions.

Clements, A. (2006). *A Million Dots.* New York: Simon & Schuster.

This book is helpful for teachers wishing to convey the concept of large numbers or even the idea of a million. The book begins with one dot and continues on to one million, but is about more than just the dots. The illustrations and text will interest the reader and teach children unique facts about unusual numbers between one and a million.

Dodds, D.A. (2005). *The Great Divide: A Mathematical Marathon.* Cambridge, MA: Candlewick.

This rhyming tale is designed to help students understand division. Although 80 people start a bike race, they don't all finish it. Along the way, they encounter obstacles that cause the number of participants to be divided again and again. There is even a surprise ending that will appeal to some readers.

Dodds, D.A. (2007). *Full House: An Invitation to Fractions.* Cambridge, MA: Candlewick.

Miss Bloom runs an inn. She loves her job and happily welcomes the guests. The reader will meet a wide range of people as guests continue to come to the inn. Eventually the inn is full for the night. However, there is a cake downstairs, and the guests are eating it. By using fractions, the reader can determine how everyone can enjoy the cake.

Dodds, D.A. (2007). *Minnie's Diner: A Multiplying Menu.* Cambridge, MA: Candlewick.

The McFay brothers have work to do, but they can't ignore their stomachs when they smell the food coming from the diner. Even though they were told to work first, one by one they go to the diner to eat. Each brother orders twice as much food as the previous sibling, providing a lesson in multiplying for young readers. After Papa heads over there to eat, Minnie has to closer her diner because she is out of food.

Einhorn, E. (2008). *A Very Improbable Story*. Watertown, MA: Charlesbridge.

> Most people do not expect a cat to teach a human about mathematics, but it happens in this text. Young readers will follow along as a cat helps explain probability to Ethan, a young boy. The cat presents Ethan with challenges and then explains the probability of certain situations occurring. As the book proceeds, the reader will learn about probability from several challenges presented to the boy. At the end of the text, the reader is introduced to two famous mathematicians credited with the concept of probability.

Fisher, D., & Sneed, D. (2008). *My Half Day*. Mount Pleasant, SC: Sylvan Dell.

> Everything in a young boy's life is a fraction. The story begins when he wakes up with half a head of hair. The story continues on by introducing the reader to a number of fractions before ending with the young boy going to bed and waking up the next day, only to find out his father's face is a clock. The boy then realizes this day must be about time. The book concludes with a variety of activities.

Fisher, V. (2006). *How High Can a Dinosaur Count? And Other Math Mysteries*. New York: Schwartz & Wade.

> This book contains 15 different math mysteries. Each mystery is a math word problem with the text on one page and the illustration on the next. Sometimes the reader will need to use clues in the illustration such as a clock to help figure out the answer to the word problems. At the back of the book, the author provides four more questions that can be asked for each mystery.

Franco, B. (2007). *Birdsongs*. New York: Margaret K. McElderry.

> In this book, the reader counts backward from 10 to 1. Each number is represented by the sound heard from a different type of bird. The book begins with a red-capped woodpecker that goes "tat" 10 times and ends with a tiny hummingbird that goes "tzik." At the end of the book, the author includes facts about each of the birds mentioned.

Franco, B. (2008). *Bees, Snails, & Peacock Tails: Patterns & Shapes... Naturally*. New York: Margaret K. McElderry.

> Through this text, the reader is introduced to a variety of shapes and patterns seen in nature. The reader learns that there are hexagons in a beehive and that migrating birds form a wedge to fly with less effort. The reader also learns that a diamond pattern can be seen on diamondback and copperhead snakes. The educational value of this book is not limited to geometry. In addition, the text provides a great deal of information about the different aspects of nature discussed

within its pages. To ensure accuracy of information, the author notes that a naturalist was consulted for this text.

Franco, B. (2009). *Zero Is the Leaves on the Tree*. Berkeley, CA: Tricycle.

This picture book teaches young students about a very difficult concept to grasp, zero. It relates zero to images and ideas with which students will be familiar. When the children in the book are all playing basketball and baseball at recess, zero is the number of balls left in the bin. Zero is also the number of ripples in a pool before anyone jumps in. The concept of zero is shown in many different ways.

Fromental, J.-L. (2006). *365 Penguins*. New York: Abrams.

It all begins on New Year's Day when a family receives a penguin. They don't know why the penguin is there, and life is about to get even stranger. Every day of the year, the family gets a new penguin. The reader is introduced to a number of mathematical concepts. Along with learning how many days are in each month, the reader is introduced to multiplication and other concepts. If the family wants to store the penguins, they might put the penguins in groups of a dozen, or perhaps they should put them in the formation of a cube. Students often enjoy looking for one penguin that stands out throughout the book.

Goldstone, B. (2008). *Greater Estimations*. New York: Henry Holt.

This book is not just about guessing or estimating, but rather it also shows the reader how to make good estimations. Although students in class may want to glance at a picture or a container of objects to estimate the contents just by looking at it, this book shows readers how to make better estimates regarding a number of mathematical concepts. Length, volume, and area estimates are all discussed.

Harris, T. (2007). *20 Hungry Piggies: A Number Book*. Minneapolis, MN: Millbrook.

In this book, 20 little piggies get together for a picnic. The story is told in verse and reinforces counting from 1 to 20. Many students will enjoy that the story mirrors the familiar five piggies tale that many of them have heard for years. The story begins with the first piggy going to the market and continues on through piggy number five, who lets the reader know "we, we, we" still have more piggies to meet. Then the readers meet 15 piggy friends one by one along with a familiar animal, the wolf. If the readers look closely, the wolf or part of the wolf is seen in every picture.

Harris, T. (2008). *Splitting the Herd: A Corral of Odds and Evens*. Minneapolis, MN: Millbrook.

This story reinforces the concept of odd and even numbers. Every time that Cowboy Kirby's cows get into Emma's yard, he counts them up and lets her keep the even ones. It is quickly apparent that math is not Cowboy Kirby's strong point. In the end, the readers learn that Cowboy Kirby and Emma are getting married, so the cows will all stay together. Then the reader is told that now the cows will multiply. Some students might want that explained.

Kroll, V.L. (2005). *Equal Schmequal*. Watertown, MA: Charlesbridge.

When a group of friends want to play tug-of-war, they realize they need to have equal sides. That is when the problem begins. How can two sides be equal? The group tries to divide up in a number of ways, but none of the ways produces equal sides for tug-of-war. Finally, they decide to use a teeter-totter to make sure that each side is equal for the game. The author explains various definitions for the concept of equal at the end of the book.

Lee, C., & O'Reilly, G. (2007). *The Great Number Rumble: A Story of Math in Surprising Places*. Toronto, ON, Canada: Annick.

Many students will find a situation in this text that they often wish would occur in their school. The entire school district has decided to no longer teach mathematics. It isn't just the students that are ecstatic. The teachers are pretty happy, too. However, while everyone is happy and celebrating, one student, Sam, who loves mathematics is not happy. He seeks to explain why math is important and fun. Through his explanation, the reader is introduced to numerous uses for math in the world and some famous mathematicians. In the end, Sam has apparently proven his case.

Leedy, L. (2007). *It's Probably Penny*. New York: Henry Holt.

This book features Lisa, a little girl, and her lovable Boston terrier. The teacher in the book is teaching about probability, and Lisa applies the mathematical concept to life with her dog. She thinks about what might happen, what can't happen, and what will happen. One of the questions Lisa ponders is whether Penny will want to go for a walk. If Penny goes on a walk, what might happen and what won't happen on the walk?

Leedy, L. (2008). *Missing Math: A Number Mystery*. New York: Marshall Cavendish.

Through the pages of this text, students realize the importance of numbers in the world around them. After a thief manages to steal all of the numbers in the town, a detective must try to solve the crime. Eventually, the problem is solved. The story is told in rhyme and contains animal characters.

McCallum, A. (2005). *The Secret Life of Math: Discover How (and Why) Numbers Have Survived From the Cave Dwellers to Us!* Nashville, TN: Williamson Books.

> This book, which is divided into three parts, can serve as a resource for the teacher, be used in a classroom library, or be shared in short sections with the class. A lot of interesting information is provided for math trivia lovers. There are a number of fun activities and projects that students can complete to make the mathematical learning even more relevant.

Napoli, D.J. (2007). *The Wishing Club: A Story About Fractions.* New York: Henry Holt.

> Four young children see a star in the sky and each individually wish for something. To their surprise, they only get a fraction of what they asked for in their wishes. They try to decide what they can do about it. The four children decide that it might be better to combine their wishes into one wish, a pet. That way they might get a whole wish instead of a fraction of a wish.

Neuschwander, C. (2005). *Mummy Math: An Adventure in Geometry.* New York: Henry Holt.

> In this book, Matt and Bibi, two familiar characters in Neuschwander's books, head off on another adventure with their parents. This time the trip is to Egypt. When the two children accidentally get stuck in the pyramid, the adventure begins. They must use their math knowledge of geometry to get out. By relating their math knowledge to hieroglyphic clues, they are able to eventually find their way to a map so that they can escape.

Neuschwander, C. (2006). *Sir Cumference and the Isle of Immeter: A Math Adventure.* Watertown, MA: Charlesbridge.

> The story begins with Per and her cousin Radius playing a game called Inners and Edges. Soon they decide to head for the Isle of Immeter, which once belonged to Countess Areana. After solving a number of math puzzles, the island is named Perimeter in honor of Per. Neuschwander has authored story books teaching about pi, circumference, angles, and a number of other mathematical concepts.

Neuschwander, C. (2007). *Patterns in Peru: An Adventure in Patterning.* New York: Henry Holt.

> In this book, twins Matt and Bibi are going on a trip with their parents to Peru. The children really hope that they can find the Lost City, but they become separated from their parents. The book focuses on patterning and sequencing. There are some additional activities at the back of the book.

Reisberg, J.A. (2006). *Zachary Zormer: Shape Transformer*. Watertown, MA: Charlesbridge.

Zachary's teacher wants the students to bring in an object every week for a math show-and-tell. Since Zachary has trouble remembering to bring in an object, he uses his creativity to relate mathematics to something he has readily available to share. Sometimes his object is as simple as a piece of paper. There are a number of mathematical concepts covered in the book. Since readers get to listen to Zachary explain each item, they will be able to understand the concepts. Students should pay attention to the chalkboard in the classroom each week.

Robinson, E.K. (2008). *Making Cents*. Berkeley, CA: Tricycle.

Readers follow a group of children who want to build a clubhouse. By working at a variety of jobs, the kids are able to save the money necessary. Readers are introduced to American currency from coins to one-hundred-dollar bills. Furthermore, the text describes what can be seen on the front and back of each currency. At the end of the book, the author talks about three currencies that aren't mentioned such as the two-dollar bill. Changes that have occurred in American currency are discussed, and readers are told where more information can be found about the currency system.

Schnitzlein, D. (2007). *The Monster Who Did My Math*. Atlanta, GA: Peachtree.

The problem in this book is one to which many children can relate. A boy has math homework due for school, but he doesn't want to do it. Procrastination can only get him so far, and on Sunday night it is time to deal with the problem. Lucky for him, a monster appears and offers to do the homework for him. The boy is pleased when his homework is done correctly, but problems begin when he didn't learn anything from the homework. Although the boy has to deal with the contract he signed with the monster, by using math he has a chance to save himself from the contract.

Tang, G. (2005). *Math Potatoes: Mind-Stretching Brain Food*. New York: Scholastic.

In this book geared for 7- to 12-year-old children, Tang focuses on three strategies. He encourages readers to look for sums of 5 and 10, patterns and symmetries, and groups of equal size. The answers at the back of the book show the easiest way to solve each fable. This book is a follow-up to *The Grapes of Math: Mind-Stretching Math Riddles* (2001) and *Math Appeal: Mind-Stretching Math Riddles* (2003). It is the seventh book in the series.

Tang, G. (2007). *Math Fables Too: Making Science Count*. New York: Scholastic.

> After the fable of one seahorse, each fable begins with a number that is later broken down. Readers go from counting to addition as they read through the fables. Through each short fable, children learn a lot of interesting information about animals. At the end of the book, there is a page with more information about animals. This book contains many interesting words, which will help build children's vocabulary. It is geared for 3- to 6-year-old children. The author has written many other mathematical trade books that appeal to a range of grades.

Professional Resources

Books

Boaler, J. (2008). *What's Math Got to Do With It? Helping Children Learn to Love Their Least Favorite Subject—And Why It's Important for America.* New York: Viking.

Bresser, R. (2004). *Math and Literature, Grades 4–6.* Sausalito, CA: Math Solutions.

Burns, M., & Gordon, T. (2007). *About Teaching Mathematics: A K–8 Resource* (3rd ed.). Sausalito, CA: Math Solutions.

Burns, M., & Sheffield, S. (2004). *Math and Literature, Grades K–1.* Sausalito, CA: Math Solutions.

Burns, M., & Sheffield, S. (2004). *Math and Literature, Grades 2–3.* Sausalito, CA: Math Solutions.

Chapin, S.H., O'Connor, C., & Anderson, N.C. (2003). *Classroom Discussions: Using Math Talk to Help Students Learn, Grades 1–6.* Sausalito, CA: Math Solutions.

Fogelberg, E., Skalinder, C., Satz, P., Hiller, B., Bernstein, L., & Vitantonio, S. (2008). *Integrating Literacy and Math: Strategies for K–6 Teachers.* New York: Guilford.

Franco, B. (2006). *Math Poetry: Linking Language and Math in a Fresh Way.* Tucson, AZ: Good Year Books.

Hyde, A. (2006). *Comprehending Math: Adapting Reading Strategies to Teach Mathematics, K–6.* Portsmouth, NH: Heinemann.

Kajander, A. (2007). *Big Ideas for Growing Mathematicians: Exploring Elementary Math With 20 Ready-to-Go Activities.* Chicago: Zephyr.

Lilburn, P., & Sullivan, P. (2002). *Good Questions for Math Teaching: Why Ask Them and What to Ask, Grades K–6.* Sausalito, CA: Math Solutions.

Minton, L. (2007). *What If Your ABCs Were Your 123s? Building Connections Between Literacy and Math*. Thousand Oaks, CA: Corwin.

Penn, M.W. (2008). *Math & Poetry Fun With Sidney the Silly and Friends*. Vancouver, BC, Canada: Gumboot.

Petersen, J. (2004). *Math and Nonfiction, K–2*. Sausalito, CA: Math Solutions.

Simpson, J. (2005). *Circle-Time Poetry Math: Delightful Poems With Activities That Help Young Children Build Phonemic Awareness, Oral Language, and Early Math Skills*. New York: Scholastic.

Thiessen, D. (Ed.). (2004). *Exploring Mathematics Through Literature: Articles and Lessons From Prekindergarten Through Grade 8*. Reston, VA: National Council of Teachers of Mathematics.

Whitin, P., & Whitin, D.J. (2000). *Math Is Language Too: Talking and Writing in the Mathematics Classroom*. Urbana, IL: National Council of Teachers of English.

Wickett, M., Kharas, K., & Burns, M. (2002). *Lessons for Algebraic Thinking, Grades 3–5*. Sausalito, CA: Math Solutions.

Professional Journals

Language Arts is published six times per year by the National Council of Teachers of English, targeting those interested in literacy development for prekindergarten through eighth-grade students. Within its pages, educators can read about classroom practices and scholarly and theoretical information. Also, children's books and professional resources are reviewed. More information can be gained at www.ncte.org.

The Reading Teacher is published by the International Reading Association eight times each year. The publication is designed for educators working with young students through age 12. Along with articles, there are departments in each issue with information about assessment, children's books, English learners, research, teaching tips, and other topics. More information can be found at www.reading.org.

Teaching Children Mathematics is published nine times a year by the National Council of Teachers of Mathematics. Articles are geared for those interested in elementary education. Through a variety of articles and departments, a number of ideas for lessons and activities are shared. More information can be found at www.nctm.org.

REFERENCES

Al Otaiba, S., & Pappamihiel, N.E. (2005). Guidelines for using volunteer literacy tutors to support reading instruction. *Teaching Exceptional Children, 37*(6), 6–11.

Altieri, J.L. (1996). Children's written responses to multicultural texts: A look at aesthetic involvement and the focuses of aesthetically complex responses. *Reading Research and Instruction, 35*(3), 237–248.

Altieri, J.L. (2005). Creating poetry: Reinforcing mathematical concepts. *Teaching Children Mathematics, 12*(1), 18–23.

Altieri, J.L. (2008). Fictional characters with dyslexia: What are we seeing in books? *Teaching Exceptional Children, 41*(1), 48–54.

Altieri, J.L. (2009). Strengthening connections between elementary classroom mathematics and literacy. *Teaching Children Mathematics, 15*(6), 346–351.

Alvermann, D.E., Phelps, S.F., & Gillis, V.R. (2006). *Content area reading and literacy: Succeeding in today's diverse classrooms* (5th ed.). New York: Allyn & Bacon.

Anderson, C. (2000). *How's it going? A practical guide to conferring with student writers.* Portsmouth, NH: Heinemann.

Andrews, S.E. (1998). Using inclusive literature to promote positive attitudes towards disabilities. *Journal of Adolescent & Adult Literacy, 41*(6), 420–426.

Anstey, M., & Bull, G. (2006). *Teaching and learning multiliteracies: Changing times, changing literacies.* Newark, DE: International Reading Association.

Armstrong, T. (1993). *Seven kinds of smart: Identifying and developing your many intelligences.* New York: Penguin.

Armstrong, T. (1994). Multiple intelligences: Seven ways to approach curriculum. *Educational Leadership, 52*(3), 26–28.

Au, K.H. (1993). *Literacy instruction in multicultural settings.* New York: Harcourt Brace.

Becker, W.C. (1977). Teaching reading and language to the disadvantaged—What we have learned from field research. *Harvard Educational Review, 47*(4), 518–543.

Berghoff, B., & Borgmann, C.B. (2007). Imagining new possibilities with our partners in the arts. *English Education, 40*(1), 21–40.

Berghoff, B., Borgmann, C.B., & Parr, N.C. (2005). *Arts together: Steps toward transformative teacher education.* Reston, VA: National Art Education Association.

Bishop, R.S. (1992). Evaluating books by and about African-Americans. In M.V. Lindgren (Ed.), *The multicolored mirror: Cultural substance in literature for children and young adults* (pp. 31–44). Fort Atkinson, WI: Highsmith Press.

Blachowicz, C.L. (1986). Making connections: Alternatives to the vocabulary notebook. *Journal of Reading, 29*(7), 643–649.

Boyce, J.S., Alber-Morgan, S.R., & Riley, J.G. (2007). Fearless public speaking: Oral presentation activities for the elementary classroom. *Childhood Education, 83*(3), 142–150.

Braddon, K.L., Hall, N.J., & Taylor, D. (1993). *Math through children's literature: Making the NCTM standards come alive.* Englewood, CO: Teacher Ideas Press.

Brown, C.L. (2005). Equity of literacy-based math performance assessments for English language learners. *Bilingual Research Journal, 29*(2), 337–364.

Buchoff, R. (1996). Riddles: Fun with language across the curriculum. *The Reading Teacher, 49*(8), 666–671.

Capps, R., Fix, M.E., Murray, J., Ost, J., Passel, J.S., & Hernandez, S.H. (2005). *The new demography of America's schools: Immigration and the No Child Left Behind Act.* Washington, DC: Urban Institute.

Caughlan, S. (2008). Advocating for the arts in an age of multiliteracies. *Language Arts, 86*(2), 120–126.

Cazden, C.B. (2005). The value of conversations for language development and reading comprehension. *Literacy Teaching and Learning, 9*(1), 1–6.

Cecil, N.L. (1994). *For the love of language: Poetry for every learner.* Winnipeg, MB, Canada: Penguin.

Chall, J.S. (1983). *Learning to read: The great debate.* New York: McGraw-Hill.

Conley, M.W. (2007). *Content area literacy: Learners in context.* New York: Allyn & Bacon.

Crafton, L.K., Brennan, M., & Silvers, P. (2007). Critical inquiry and multiliteracies in a first-grade classroom. *Language Arts, 84*(6), 510–518.

Crespo, S.M., & Kyriakides, A.O. (2007). To draw or not to draw: Exploring children's drawings for solving mathematics problems. *Teaching Children Mathematics, 14*(2), 118–125.

Daiute, C. (1989). Play and learning to write. *Language Arts, 66*(6), 656–664.

DeRita, C., & Weaver, S. (1991). Cross-age literacy program. *Reading Improvement, 28*(4), 244–248.

DiGisi, L.L., & Fleming, D. (2005). Literacy specialists in math class! Closing the achievement gap on state math assessments. *Voices From the Middle, 13*(1), 48–52.

Drake, S.M. (1998). *Creating integrated curriculum: Proven ways to increase student learning.* Thousand Oaks, CA: Corwin.

Duffelmeyer, F.A., & Duffelmeyer, B.B. (1979). Developing vocabulary through dramatization. In N.H. Brizendine & J.L. Thomas (Eds.), *Learning through dramatics: Ideas for teachers and librarians* (pp. 58–61). Phoenix, AZ: Oryx.

Durkin, D. (1981). Reading comprehension instruction in five basal reading series. *Reading Research Quarterly, 16*(4), 515–544. doi:10.2307/747314

Dyson, A.H. (1989). *Multiple worlds of child writers: Friends learning to write.* New York: Teachers College Press.

Dyson, A.H. (2006). On saying it right (write): "Fix-its" in the foundation of learning to write. *Research in the Teaching of English, 41*(1), 8–42.

Eeds, M., & Cockrum, W.A. (1985). Teaching word meanings by expanding schemata vs. dictionary work vs. reading in context. *Journal of Reading, 28*(6), 492–497.

Eeds, M., & Wells, M. (1991). Talking, thinking and cooperative learning: Lessons learned from listening to children talk about books. *Social Education, 55*(2), 134–137.

Eisner, E.W. (2003). The arts and the creation of mind. *Language Arts, 80*(5), 340–344.

Favazza, P.C., & Odom, S.L. (1997). Promoting positive attitudes of kindergarten-age children toward people with disabilities. *Exceptional Children, 63*(3), 405–418.

Finn, P.J. (1999). *Literacy with an attitude: Educating working class children in their own interest.* Albany, NY: SUNY Press.

Fisher, C.J., & Natarella, M.A. (1982). Young children's preferences in poetry: A national survey of first, second and third graders. *Research in the Teaching of English, 16*(4), 339–354.

Fitzgerald, J. (1995). English-as-a-second-language reading instruction in the United States: A research review. *Journal of Reading Behavior, 27*(2), 115–152.

Flood, J., & Lapp, D. (1995). Broadening the lens: Toward an expanded conceptualization of literacy. In K.A. Hinchman, D.J. Leu Jr., & C.K. Kinzer (Eds.), *Perspectives on literacy research and practice* (pp. 1–16). Chicago: National Reading Conference.

Flood, J., & Lapp, D. (1998). Broadening conceptualizations of literacy: The visual and communicative arts. *The Reading Teacher, 51*(4), 342–344.

Galda, L., Bisplinghoff, B.S., Pellegrini, A.D., & Stahl, S. (1995). Sharing lives: Reading, writing, talking, and living in a first-grade classroom. *Language Arts, 72*(5), 334–339.

Gardner, H. (1987). *Frames of mind: The theory of multiple intelligences.* New York: Basic.

Gardner, H. (2006). *Multiple intelligences: New horizons.* New York: Basic.

Goldenberg, C. (1992). Instructional conversations: Promoting comprehension through discussion. *The Reading Teacher, 46*(4), 316–326.

Graves, D.H. (1983). *Writing: Teachers and children at work.* Exeter, NH: Heinemann.

Graves, D.H. (1991). Trust the shadows. *The Reading Teacher, 45*(1), 18–24.

Guthrie, J.T., Anderson, E., Alao, S., & Rinehart, J. (1999). Influences of concept-oriented reading instruction on strategy use and conceptual learning from text. *The Elementary School Journal, 99*(4), 343–366. doi:10.1086/461929

Hadaway, N.L., Vardell, S.M., & Young, T.A. (2001). Scaffolding oral language through poetry for students learning English. *The Reading Teacher, 54*(8), 796–805.

Hansen, J. (2001). *When writers read* (2nd ed.). Portsmouth, NH: Heinemann.

Hansen-Thomas, H. (2008). Sheltered instruction: Best practices for ELLs in the mainstream. *Kappa Delta Pi Record, 44*(4), 165–169.

Hargis, C.H., Terhaar-Yonkers, M., Williams, P.C., & Reed, M.T. (1988). Repetition requirements for word recognition. *Journal of Reading, 31*(4), 320–327.

Harste, J.C., Woodward, V.A., & Burke, C.L. (1984). *Language stories and literacy lessons.* Portsmouth, NH: Heinemann.

Harvey, S., & Goudvis, A. (2007). *Strategies that work: Teaching comprehension for understanding and engagement.* Portland, ME: Stenhouse.

Hellwig, S.J., Monroe, E.E., & Jacobs, J.S. (2000). Making informed choices: Selecting children's trade books for mathematics instruction. *Teaching Children Mathematics, 7*(3), 138–143.

Helman, L.A., & Burns, M.K. (2008). What does oral language have to do with it? Helping young English-language learners acquire a sight word vocabulary. *The Reading Teacher, 62*(1), 14–19. doi:10.1598/RT.62.1.2

Hickman, P., Pollard-Durodola, S., & Vaughn, S. (2004). Storybook reading: Improving vocabulary and comprehension for English-language learners. *The Reading Teacher, 57*(8), 720–730.

Hinchman, K.A., Alvermann, D.E., Boyd, F.B., Brozo, W.G., & Vacca, R.T. (2004). Supporting older students' in- and out-of-school literacies. *Journal of Adolescent & Adult Literacy, 47*(4), 304–310.

Hoff, D.J. (2001). Group issues standards on speaking, listening for preschool to 3rd grade. *Education Week, 20*(33), 11.

Hoffman, J.V., McCarthey, S.J., Abbott, J., Christian, C., Corman, L., Curry, C., et al. (1994). So what's new in the new basal? A focus on first grade. *Journal of Reading Behavior, 26*(1), 47–73.

Hopkins, G., & Bean, T.W. (1999). Vocabulary learning with the verbal-visual word association strategy in a Native American community. *Journal of Adolescent & Adult Literacy, 42*(4), 274–281.

Hunsader, P.D. (2004). Mathematics trade books: Establishing their value and assessing their quality. *The Reading Teacher, 57*(7), 618–629.

Ikpeze, C.H., & Boyd, F.B. (2007). Web-based inquiry learning: Facilitating thoughtful literacy with WebQuests. *The Reading Teacher, 60*(7), 644–654. doi:10.1598/RT.60.7.5

International Reading Association & National Council of Teachers of English. (1996). *Standards for the English language arts.* Newark, DE; Urbana, IL: Authors.

Kiefer, B., Hepler, S., & Hickman, J. (2006). *Charlotte Huck's children's literature* (9th ed.). New York: McGraw-Hill.

Koch, K. (1970). *Wishes, lies, and dreams: Teaching children to write poetry.* New York: Chelsea House.

Kress, G.R. (2003). *Literacy in the new media age.* London: Routledge.

Kristeva, J. (1984). *Revolution in poetic language.* New York: Columbia University Press.

Kutiper, K., & Wilson, P. (1993). Updating poetry preferences: A look at the poetry children really like. *The Reading Teacher, 47*(1), 28–35.

Lancia, P.J. (1997). Literary borrowing: The effects of literature on children's writing. *The Reading Teacher, 50*(6), 470–475.

Leland, C.H., & Harste, J.C. (1994). Multiple ways of knowing: Curriculum in a new key. *Language Arts, 71*(5), 337–345.

Leu, D.J., Jr. (2000). Literacy and technology: Deictic consequences for literacy education in an information age. In M.L. Kamil, P.B. Mosenthal, P.D. Pearson, & R. Barr (Eds.), *Handbook of reading research* (Vol. 3, pp. 743–770). Mahwah, NJ: Erlbaum.

Liu, Z. (2005). Reading behavior in the digital environment: Changes in reading behavior over the past ten years. *The Journal of Documentation, 61*(6), 700–712. doi:10.1108/00220410510632040

Loban, W. (1976). *Language development: Kindergarten through grade twelve* (Research Report No. 18). Urbana, IL: National Council of Teachers of English.

Lopez, E.M., Gallimore, R., Garnier, H., & Reese, L. (2007). Preschool antecedents of mathematics achievement of Latinos: The influence of family resources, early literacy experiences, and preschool attendance. *Hispanic Journal of Behavioral Sciences, 29*(4), 456–471. doi:10.1177/0739986307305910

Maloch, B., Hoffman, J.V., & Patterson, E.U. (2004). Local texts: Reading and writing "of the classroom." In J.V. Hoffman & D.L. Schallert (Eds.), *The texts in elementary classrooms* (pp. 145–156). Mahwah, NJ: Erlbaum.

McKeown, M.G., Beck, I.L., Omanson, R.C., & Perfetti, C.A. (1983). The effects of long-term vocabulary instructions on reading comprehension: A replication. *Journal of Reading Behavior, 15*(1), 3–18.

McMaster, J.C. (1998). "Doing" literature: Using drama to build literacy. *The Reading Teacher, 51*(7), 574–584.

McPherson, K. (2007). New online technologies for new literacy instruction. *Teacher Librarian, 34*(3), 69–71.

Moje, E.B. (2008). Foregrounding the disciplines in secondary literacy teaching and learning: A call for change. *Journal of Adolescent & Adult Literacy, 52*(2), 96–107. doi:10.1598/JAAL.52.2.1

Moje, E.B., Overby, M., Tysvaer, N., & Morris, K. (2008). The complex world of adolescent literacy: Myths, motivations, and mysteries. *Harvard Educational Review, 78*(1), 107–154.

Moll, L.C. (Ed.). (1990). *Vygotsky and education: Instructional implications and applications of sociohistorical psychology.* New York: Cambridge University Press.

Moore, D.W., Moore, S.A., Cunningham, P.M., & Cunningham, J.W. (2006). *Developing readers and writers in the content areas K–12* (5th ed.). New York: Allyn & Bacon.

Moran, S., Kornhaber, M., & Gardner, H. (2006). Orchestrating multiple intelligences. *Educational Leadership, 64*(1), 22–27.

Moyer, P.S. (2000). Communicating mathematically: Children's literature as a natural connection. *The Reading Teacher, 54*(3), 246–256.

Nagy, W.E. (1988). *Teaching vocabulary to improve reading comprehension.* Newark, DE: International Reading Association.

Nahrang, C.L., & Peterson, B.T. (1986). Using writing to learn mathematics. *Mathematics Teacher, 79*(6), 461–465.

National Center for Education Statistics. (2002). *Internet access in U.S. public schools and classrooms: 1994–2001.* Retrieved October 28, 2008, from www.nces.ed.gov/pubs2002/Internet

National Council of Teachers of Mathematics. (2000). *Principles and standards for school mathematics.* Reston, VA: Author.

Neeld, E.C., & Kiefer, K. (1990). *Writing* (3rd ed.). Glenview, IL: Scott Foresman.

Norton, D.E. (1990). Teaching multicultural literature in the reading curriculum. *The Reading Teacher, 44*(1), 28–40.

Norton, D.E., & Norton, S.E. (2002). *Through the eyes of a child: An introduction to children's literature* (6th ed.). Upper Saddle River, NJ: Prentice Hall.

Nuthall, G. (1999). The way students learn: Acquiring knowledge from an integrated science and social studies unit. *The Elementary School Journal, 99*(4), 303–341. doi:10.1086/461928

Nystrand, M., Gamoran, A., & Heck, M.J. (1993). Using small groups for response to and thinking about literature. *English Journal, 82*(1), 14–22. doi:10.2307/820670

Perkins, D. (1988). Art as understanding. *Journal of Aesthetic Education, 22*(1), 111–131. doi:10.2307/3332969

Piro, J.M. (2002). The picture of reading: Deriving meaning in literacy through image. *The Reading Teacher, 56*(2), 126–134.

Pugalee, D.K. (1997). Connecting writing to the mathematics curriculum. *Mathematics Teacher, 90*(4), 308–310.

Rankin, J.L. (1992). Connecting literacy learners: A pen pal project. *The Reading Teacher, 46*(3), 204–214.

Readence, J.E., Bean, T.W., & Baldwin, R.S. (1998). *Content area literacy: An integrated approach* (6th ed.). Dubuque, IA: Kendall/Hunt.

Rief, L. (2003). Quick-writes: Leads to literacy. *Voices From the Middle, 10*(1), 50–51.

Rinehart, S.D. (1999). "Don't think for a minute that I'm getting up there": Opportunities for readers' theater in a tutorial for children with reading problems. *Reading Psychology, 20*(1), 71–89. doi:10.1080/027027199278510

Robb, L. (1999). 3 strategies for getting the most from textbooks. *Instructor, 112*(5), 36–39.

Rosenblatt, L.M. (1978). *The reader, the text, the poem: The transactional theory of literary work*. Carbondale: Southern Illinois University Press.

Ross, E.P., & Roe, B.D. (1977). Creative drama builds proficiency in reading. In N.H. Brizendine & J.L. Thomas (Eds.), *Learning through dramatics: Ideas for teachers and librarians* (pp. 52–57). Phoenix, AZ: Oryx.

Routman, R. (2000). *Kids' poems: Teaching first graders to love writing poetry*. New York: Scholastic.

Sarama, J., & Clements, D.H. (2003). Building blocks of early childhood mathematics. *Teaching Children Mathematics, 9*(8), 480–484.

Schiro, M. (1997). *Integrating children's literature and mathematics in the classroom: Children as meaning makers, problem solvers, and literary critics*. New York: Teachers College Press.

Schwartz, R.M., & Raphael, T.E. (1985). Concept of definition: A key to improving students' vocabulary. *The Reading Teacher, 39*(2), 198–205.

Sheridan-Thomas, H.K. (2007). Making sense of multiple literacies: Exploring pre-service content area teachers' understandings and applications. *Reading Research and Instruction, 46*(2), 121–150.

Short, K.G., Harste, J.C., & Burke, C.L. (1996). *Creating classrooms for authors and inquirers* (2nd ed.). Portsmouth, NH: Heinemann.

Sidelnick, M.A., & Svoboda, M.L. (2000). The bridge between drawing and writing: Hannah's story. *The Reading Teacher, 54*(2), 174–184.

Silver, J.W. (1999). A survey on the use of writing-to-learn in mathematics classes. *Mathematics Teacher, 92*(5), 388–390.

Smith, J.A., & Bowers, P.S. (1989). Approaches to using literature for teaching reading. *Reading Improvement, 26*(4), 345–348.

Smolin, L.I., & Lawless, K.A. (2003). Becoming literate in the technological age: New responsibilities and tools for teachers. *The Reading Teacher, 56*(6), 570–577.

Sneed, J. (1995). "Drawing" on knowledge. *The Reading Teacher, 48*(7), 585.

Spina, S.U. (2006). Worlds together...words apart: An assessment of the effectiveness of arts-based curriculum for second language learners. *Journal of Latinos and Education, 5*(2), 99–122. doi:10.1207/s1532771xjle0502_3

Strickland, D.S., & Morrow, L.M. (1988). New perspectives on young children learning to read and write. *The Reading Teacher, 42*(1), 70–71.

Taba, H. (1967). *Teacher's handbook for elementary social studies*. Reading, MA: Addison-Wesley.

Tanner, M.L., & Casados, L. (1998). Promoting and studying discussions in math classes. *Journal of Adolescent & Adult Literacy, 41*(5), 342–350.

Tompkins, G.E. (2009). *Language arts: Patterns of practice* (9th ed.). Upper Saddle River, NJ: Pearson Education.

Tyler, B.J., & Chard, D.J. (2000). Using Readers Theatre to foster fluency in struggling readers: A twist on the repeated reading strategy. *Reading & Writing Quarterly, 16*(2), 163–168. doi:10.1080/105735600278015

U.S. Census Bureau. (2001). *Statistical abstract of the United States: 2000* (population section). Washington, DC: U.S. Department of Commerce, Economics and Statistics Administration.

Vacca, J.A.L., Vacca, R.T., & Gove, M.K. (1987). *Reading and learning to read*. Boston: Little, Brown.

Vygotsky, L.S. (1962). *Thought and language.* Cambridge, MA: MIT Press.

Vygotsky, L.S. (1978). *Mind in society: The development of higher psychological processes* (M. Cole, V. John-Steiner, S. Scribner, & E. Souberman, Eds. & Trans.). Cambridge, MA: Harvard University Press. (Original work published 1934)

White, T.G., Graves, M.F., & Slater, W.H. (1990). Development of recognition and reading vocabularies in diverse sociolinguistic and educational settings. *Journal of Educational Psychology, 82*(2), 281–290. doi:10.1037/0022-0663.82.2.281

Williams, B.T. (2008). "Tomorrow will not be like today": Literacy and identity in a world of multiliteracies. *Journal of Adult & Adolescent Literacy, 51*(8), 682–686. doi:10.1598/JAAL.51.8.7

Williams, T.L. (2007). "Reading" the painting: Exploring visual literacy in the primary grades. *The Reading Teacher, 60*(7), 636–642. doi:10.1598/RT.60.7.4

Wolvin, A.D., & Coakley, C.G. (1996). *Listening* (5th ed.). New York: McGraw-Hill.

Woodward, A. (1986). Over-programmed materials: Taking the teacher out of teaching. *American Education, 10*(1), 26–31.

LITERATURE CITED

Adler, D.A. (2000). *Shape up!* New York: Holiday House.

Burns, M. (2008). *The greedy triangle.* New York: Scholastic.

Christelow, E. (2007). *Five little monkeys go shopping.* New York: Clarion.

Cleary, B.P. (2003). *Under, over, by the clover: What is a preposition?* Minneapolis, MN: Millbrook.

Cleary, B.P. (2008). *On the scale, a weighty tale.* Minneapolis, MN: Millbrook.

Curtis, J.L. (1995). *When I was little: A four-year-old's memoir of her youth.* New York: HarperTrophy.

Ehlert, L. (1990). *Fish eyes: A book you can count on.* New York: Trumpet.

Esham, B. (2008). *Last to finish: A story about the smartest boy in math class.* Ocean City, MD: Mainstream Connections.

Fisher, D., & Sneed, D. (2006). *One odd day.* Mount Pleasant, SC: Sylvan Dell.

Fisher, D., & Sneed, D. (2007). *My even day.* Mount Pleasant, SC: Sylvan Dell.

Fleischman, P. (2008). *Big talk: Poems for four voices.* Cambridge, MA: Candlewick.

Franco, B. (2003). *Mathematickles!* New York: Aladdin.

Franco, B. (2006). *Math poetry: Linking language and math in a fresh way.* Tucson, AZ: Good Year.

Gifford, S. (2003). *Piece = part = portion: Fractions = decimals = percents.* Berkeley, CA: Tricycle.

Giganti, P. (1999). *Each orange had 8 slices: A counting book.* New York: HarperCollins.

Gwynne, F. (2005). *A chocolate moose for dinner.* New York: Aladdin.

Gwynne, F. (2006). *The king who rained.* New York: Aladdin.

Harris, T. (2008). *Jenny found a penny.* Minneapolis, MN: Millbrook.

Heller, R. (1998). *Behind the mask: A book about prepositions.* New York: Putnam.

Hillman, B. (2007). *How big is it? A big book all about BIGness.* New York: Scholastic.

Hoberman, M.A. (2001). *You read to me, I'll read to you: Very short stories to read together.* New York: Little, Brown.

Hoberman, M.A. (2004). *You read to me, I'll read to you: Very short fairy tales to read together.* New York: Little, Brown.

Hoberman, M.A. (2007). *You read to me, I'll read to you: Very short scary tales to read together.* New York: Little, Brown.

Hopkins, L.B. (Ed.). (2001). *Marvelous math: A book of poems.* New York: Aladdin.

Leedy, L. (2000). *Measuring Penny.* New York: Henry Holt.

Lewis, J.P. (1996). *Riddle-icious.* New York: Dragonfly.

Lewis, J.P. (2002). *Arithme-tickle: An even number of odd riddle-rhymes.* New York: Silver Whistle.

Mariconda, B. (2008). *Sort it out!* Mount Pleasant, SC: Sylvan Dell.

Martin, B., & Archambault, J. (2000). *Chicka chicka boom boom.* New York: Aladdin.

Martin, B., & Sampson, M. (2004). *Chicka chicka 1, 2, 3.* New York: Simon & Schuster.

Martin, J. (2003). *ABC math riddles.* Columbus, NC: Peel Productions.

Monroe, E.E. (2006). *Math dictionary: The easy, simple, fun guide to help math phobics become math lovers.* Honesdale, PA: Boyds Mills.

Murphy, S.J. (2005). *Polly's pen pal.* New York: HarperCollins.

Neuschwander, C. (1999). *Sir Cumference and the first round table: A math adventure.* Watertown, MA: Charlesbridge.

Pappas, T. (1993). *Math talk: Mathematical ideas in poems for two voices.* San Carlos, CA: Wide World Publishing/Tetra.

Pinczes, E.J. (1999). *One hundred hungry ants.* Boston: Houghton Mifflin.

Schwartz, D.M. (1998). *G is for googol: A math alphabet book.* New York: Scholastic.

Schwartz, D.M. (2003). *Millions to measure.* New York: HarperCollins.

Simpson, J. (2005). *Circle-time poetry math: Delightful poems with activities that help young children build phonemic awareness, oral language, and early math skills.* New York: Scholastic.

Sloat, T. (1995). *From one to one hundred.* New York: Puffin.

Tang, G. (2002). *Math for all seasons.* New York: Scholastic.

Terban, M. (2007a). *Eight ate: A feast of homonym riddles.* New York: Clarion.

Terban, M. (2007b). *How much can a bare bear bear? What are homonyms and homophones?* Minneapolis, MN: First Avenue Editions.

Thong, R. (2000). *Round is a mooncake: A book of shapes.* New York: Scholastic.

Turner, P. (1999). *Among the odds & evens: A tale of adventure.* New York: Scholastic.

Viorst, J. (1978). *Alexander, who used to be rich last Sunday.* New York: Atheneum.

Walton, R. (2001). *One more bunny: Adding from one to ten.* New York: Scholastic.

Wood, A. (1991). *The napping house.* New York: Harcourt Big Books.

Zaslavsky, C. (2003). *More math games & activities from around the world.* Chicago: Chicago Review.

INDEX

Note: Page numbers followed by f and t indicate figures and tables, respectively.

A

ABC Math Riddles (Martin), 23, 82–83
ABC poems, 75–76
academic language, social language compared to, 95–96, 128
accuracy of content, 28
Adler, D.A., 82, 169
admit slips, 51–54
advertisements, persuasive, 148–149, 150f, 151
aesthetic listening, 97
Alao, S., 5
Alber-Morgan, S.R., 100
Alexander, Who Use to Be Rich Last Sunday (Viorst), 24
Al Otaiba, S., 14–15
Altieri, J.L., 33, 76
Alvermann, D.E., 5, 131, 134
Among the Odds & Evens (Turner), 24
Anderson, C., 66
Anderson, E., 5
Andrews, S.E., 33
Anstey, M., 130
application of knowledge outside classrooms, using quick-writes for, 48–49
Archambault, J., 22
Arithme-Tickle (Lewis), 23, 80
Armstrong, T., 133, 160
arts, and literacy, 132–133, 135, 162
assessment: literacy-mathematics connection and, xiii–xiv; preparation for, 13; through poetry, 93. *See also* standards for content areas
Au, K.H., 95, 101
authentic learning experiences, provision of, 13–14
award winning children's literature, 26–27

B

Baldwin, R.S., 146
Ball, J., 169
basal series, 18
Bean, T.W., 146
Beck, I.L., 78
Becker, W.C., 78
Bees, Snails, & Peacock Tails (Franco), 171–172
Berghoff, B., 130, 162
Big Talk (Fleischman), 87
Birdsongs (Franco), 171
Bishop, R.S., 33
Bisplinghoff, B.S., 100
Blachowicz, C.L., 109
Boaler, J., 5
booklist selections of children's literature, 26–27
books, for professionals, 177–178
Borgmann, C.B., 130, 162
Bowers, P.S., 20
Boyce, J.S., 100
Boyd, F.B., 131, 134, 136
Braddon, K.L., 20
brainstorming activity, with cubing, 63–64
breaking day and curriculum into parts, 7
Brennan, M., 130
Brown, C.L., 15
Brozo, W.G., 131, 134
Buchoff, R., 80
Bull, G., 130
Burke, C.L., 134, 161–162
Burns, M., 55, 169
Burns, M.K., 134, 135

C

Caldecott Medal winners, 26
Calvert, P., 170
Capps, R., 15
Casados, L., 18, 69

CAUGHLAN, S., 131
CAZDEN, C.B., 95
CECIL, N.L., 70
CHALL, J.S., 18
CHARACTERS, EVALUATION OF, 31
CHARD, D.J., 161
CHILDREN'S CHOICES BOOKLIST, 26–27
CHILDREN'S LITERATURE: award winners and booklist selections, 26–27; genres of, for development of mathematical understandings, 20–25; incorporation of, into classroom, 18; literary criteria for selection of, 31–33; mathematical criteria for selection of, 27–30; selection of, 25–26
CHRISTELOW, E., 26
CIRCLE DISCUSSIONS, 101
CIRCLE-TIME POETRY MATH (SIMPSON), 23
CLASS POEMS, CREATING, 73
CLASS TRADE BOOKS, CREATING, 151–154, 153f
CLEARY, B.P., 47, 85
CLEMENTS, A., 170
CLEMENTS, D.H., 132–133
CLOSURE, BRINGING TO LESSON WITH QUICK-WRITES, 47–48
COAKLEY, C.G., 96
COCKRUM, W.A., 146
COLLABORATION BETWEEN STUDENTS, FACILITATION OF, 12–13
COMMUNICATION STANDARD (NCTM), 9, 44, 69–70, 167
COMMUNITY INVOLVEMENT, ENCOURAGEMENT OF, 14–15
COMMUNITY OF LEARNERS, CREATION OF, 100
COMPREHENSION: of nonverbal behavior, 96–97; of visual media, 130
CONCEPT BOOKS, 21–22
CONCEPT CIRCLES, 102, 103f, 104–105
CONCEPT OF DEFINITION, 105–106, 107f
CONCEPTS, VISUAL REPRESENTATIONS OF, 139–143, 141f, 142f
CONLEY, M.W., 5
CONNECTIONS STANDARD (NCTM), 9, 168
CONTENT AREA INTEGRATION, ix–x, 5–7, 16–17
CONTENT AREA STANDARDS: commonalities of, 9–11; technology incorporation and, 10–11

COUNTING BOOKS, 22
CRAFTON, L.K., 130
CREATIVE WRITING, 54–55, 58–59
CRESPO, S.M., 152, 153
CRITERIA FOR EVALUATION OF BOOKS: literary, 31–33; mathematical, 27–30
CRITICAL LISTENING, 98
CUBING, 61–65
CULTURAL DIVERSITY, 15–16
CULTURAL VALUES, EVALUATION OF, 33
CUNNINGHAM, J.W., 5
CUNNINGHAM, P.M., 5
CURRICULAR MATERIALS: choice of, 19–20, 21; print media, 34–38. See also children's literature
CURRICULAR PLAN ACROSS GRADE LEVELS, 25
CURTIS, J.L., 76–77

D

DAIUTE, C., 126
DEBATES, 118–121
DeRITA, C., 158
DEVELOPMENTAL APPROPRIATENESS OF CONTENT, 29–30, 32
DiGISI, L.L., 15
DISCRIMINATIVE LISTENING, 96–97
DIVERSITY, CULTURAL AND LINGUISTIC, 15–16
DODDS, D.A., 170
DRAKE, S.M., 16
DRAMATIC REPRESENTATIONS, 158–161
DRAWING, TYPES AND USES OF, 152–154
DUFFELMEYER, B.B., 159
DUFFELMEYER, F.A., 159
DURKIN, D., 18
DYSON, A.H., 43, 95

E

EACH ORANGE HAD 8 SLICES (GIGANTI), 151
EEDS, M., 69, 146
EFFERENT LISTENING, 97–98
EHLERT, L., 22, 32
EINHORN, E., 171
EISNER, E.W., 132, 133
ENGLISH LEARNERS (ELs): homonyms and, 144, 145; mathematical conversations in home and, 100; recommendations for, 15–16; scaffolding for, 134–135

Equal Schmequal (Kroll), 173
Esham, B., 24
ethical values, evaluation of, 33
evaluation of books: award winners and booklist selections, 26–27; literary criteria for, 31–33; mathematical criteria for, 27–30; overview of, 25–26
exit slips, 51–54
expectations for activities, setting realistic, 126

F

Favazza, P.C., 33
Finn, P.J., 136
Fish Eyes (Ehlert), 22
Fisher, C.J., 70
Fisher, D., 27, 28, 171
Fisher, V., 171
Fitzgerald, J., 13
Five Little Monkeys Go Shopping (Christelow), 26
Fleischman, P., 87
Fleming, D., 15
flexibility during activities, 126
Flood, J., 129, 134
fluent reading, modeling, 72
focused mathematical communication: concept circles, 102, 103f, 104–105; concept of definition, 105–106, 107f; "Got It!" activity, 113–114; knowledge ratings, 108–111, 110f; list-group-label strategy, 111–113; overview of, 101–102; trivia hunt, 114–115; Venn diagrams, 107–108, 108f
formal mathematical talk: debates, 118–121; interviews, 121–124; moving students to, 116–118; overview of, 116; raps and plays, 124–125
formula poetry: ABC poems, 75–76; "I Don't Understand" poems, 78–80; "...Is" poems, 70–75; "I used to Think..., but Now I Know" poems, 76–78; overview of, 70
Franco, B., 23, 27, 71–72, 171–172
From One to One Hundred (Sloat), 81
Fromental, J.-L., 172
Full House (Dodds), 170

G

G Is for Googol (Schwartz), 24
Galda, L., 100
Gallimore, R., 15
Gamoran, A., 12–13
Gardner, H., 16, 133, 158
Garnier, H., 15
genres of literature for development of mathematical understandings, 20–25
Gifford, S., 21
Giganti, P., 151
Gillis, V.R., 5
Go Figure (Ball), 169
goals of literacy education, 4
Goldenberg, C., 99
Goldstone, B., 172
"Got It!" activity, 113–114
Goudvis, A., 5–6
Gove, M.K., 102
grade levels: curricular plan across, 25; pen pal letter writing and, 60–61
graphics, evaluation of, 32
Graves, D.H., 43
Graves, M.F., 78
The Great Divide (Dodds), 170
The Great Number Rumble (Lee & O'Reilly), 173
Greater Estimations (Goldstone), 172
The Greedy Triangle (Burns), 55
groups: concept of definition and, 106; cubing activity and, 62, 63; importance of work in, 69; journal writing and, 51; math mysteries and, 104–105; writing roulette and, 55–58
Guthrie, J.T., 5
Gwynne, F., 144

H

Hadaway, N.L., 92
Hall, N.J., 20
Hansen, J., 68
Hansen-Thomas, H., 15
Hargis, C.H., 135
Harris, T., 88, 172–173
Harste, J.C., 7, 13, 132, 134, 161–162
Harvey, S., 5–6
Heck, M.J., 12–13

HELLER, R., 85
HELMAN, L.A., 134, 135
HEPLER, S., 20, 92
HICKMAN, J., 20, 92
HICKMAN, P., 101
HILLMAN, B., 26
HINCHMAN, K.A., 131, 134
HOBERMAN, M.A., 89
HOFF, D.J., 95
HOFFMAN, J.V., 18, 19, 34, 35–37
HOMONYMS, 143–144
HOMOPHONES, 143, 144
HOPKINS, G., 146
HOPKINS, L.B., 23, 70, 71–72
How Big Is It? (HILLMAN), 26
How High Can a Dinosaur Count? (FISHER),
    171
HUNSADER, P.D., 25, 27, 30–31

I

"I Don't Understand" POEMS, 78–80
"I used to Think..., but Now I Know" POEMS,
    76–78
ICONIC DRAWINGS, 152
IKPEZE, C.H., 136
ILLUSTRATIONS, EVALUATION OF, 32
IMPORTED TEXTS: definition of, 19–20; types
    of, 38t; uses of, 37–38
INFORMAL DRAMA ACTIVITIES, 158–160
INFORMATIONAL BOOKS, 24–25
INFORMATIONAL WRITING: cubing, 61–65;
    overview of, 59; pen pal letters, 60–61
INSTRUCTIONAL FEASIBILITY, ENHANCEMENT OF,
    12, 30
INTEGRATED LEARNING. *See* content area
    integration
INTELLECTUAL APPROPRIATENESS OF CONTENT,
    29–30
INTELLIGENCES, TYPES OF, 133
INTERNATIONAL READING ASSOCIATION (IRA), xi,
    4, 7, 19, 33, 44, 69, 94, 100, 115, 129,
    133, 137
INTERNET ACCESS, 11, 136
INTERVIEWS, 121–124
"...Is" POEMS, 70–75
It's Probably Penny (LEEDY), 173

J

JOURNALS, PROFESSIONAL, 178–179
JOURNAL WRITING, 50–51

K

KIEFER, B., 20, 92
KIEFER, K., 59, 61, 62
KNOWLEDGE, APPLICATION OF OUTSIDE
    CLASSROOMS, USING QUICK-WRITES FOR,
    48–49
KNOWLEDGE RATINGS, 108–111, 110f
KOCH, K., 76
KORNHABER, M., 16, 133
KRESS, G.R., 131
KRISTEVA, J., 134
KROLL, V.L., 173
KUTIPER, K., 70
KYRIAKIDES, A.O., 152, 153

L

LANCIA, P.J., 68
Language Arts (JOURNAL), 178
LAPP, D., 129, 134
Last to Finish (ESHAM), 24
LAWLESS, K.A., 11, 129–130, 136
LEE, C., 173
LEEDY, L., 23, 173
LELAND, C.H., 7, 13, 132, 134
LENGTH OF FORMULA POETRY, 74–75
LEU, D.J., JR., 136
LEWIS, J.P., 23, 80
LINGUISTIC DIVERSITY, 15–16
LISTENING SKILLS: aesthetic, 97; critical, 98;
    discriminative, 96–97; efferent, 97–98;
    guidelines for, 125–127; interviews and,
    121–124; overview of, 3–4, 95–96
LIST-GROUP-LABEL STRATEGY, 111–113
LITERACY: aspects of, 5; benefits of changing
    view of, 132–136; broad view of, xi, xiii,
    7; content area, 5–6; definition of, 3–5;
    multiliteracies, value of, 130–131; out-of-
    school, enhancement of, 135
LITERACY-MATHEMATICS CONNECTION:
    assessments and, xiii–xiv; barriers
    to, 5–7; benefits of building, 12–16;
    limited view of, xi; reading for authentic
    purposes and, 19; strengthening, ix–x

LOBAN, W., 4, 127

LOCAL TEXTS: definition of, 19; incorporation of, 34–35; types of, 35, 38t; uses of, 35–38

LOPEZ, E.M., 15

M

MAKING CENTS (ROBINSON), 175

MALOCH, B., 19, 34, 35–37

MARICONDA, B., 28

MARTIN, B., 22

MARTIN, J., 23, 82–83

MARVELOUS MATH (HOPKINS), 23, 70

MATH DICTIONARY (MONROE), 28

MATH FABLES TOO (TANG), 175

MATH FOR ALL SEASONS (TANG), 80

MATH MYSTERIES, SOLVING, 102, 103f, 104–105

MATH POETRY (FRANCO), 27

MATH POTATOES (TANG), 175

MATH TALK (PAPPAS), 87–88

MATHEMATICAL CONVERSATIONS, INFORMAL, 98–100

MATHEMATICAL TRADE BOOKS. *See* trade books

MATHEMATICKLES! (FRANCO), 23

MCCALLUM, A., 174

MCKEOWN, M.G., 78

MCMASTER, J.C., 158, 159

MCPHERSON, K., 135–136

MEASUREMENT STANDARD (NCTM), 46

MEASURING PENNY (LEEDY), 23

MEDIA: print, 34–38; viewing, 129–136

METRIC SYSTEM, AND QUICK-WRITES, 46–47

A MILLION DOTS (CLEMENTS), 170

MILLIONS TO MEASURE (SCHWARTZ), 46

MINNIE'S DINER (DODDS), 170

MISSING MATH (LEEDY), 173

MODELING FLUENT READING, 72

MOJE, E.B., 7, 131

MOLL, L.C., 20

MONROE, E.E., 28

THE MONSTER WHO DID MY MATH (SCHNITZLEIN), 175

MOORE, D.W., 5

MOORE, S.A., 5

MORAN, S., 16, 133

MORE MATH GAMES & ACTIVITIES FROM AROUND THE WORLD (ZASLAVSKY), 25

MORRIS, K., 131

MORROW, L.M., 43

MOTIVATION, FACILITATION OF, 30

MOYER, P.S., 6, 21

MULTIETHNIC LITERATURE, 33

MULTILITERACIES, VALUE OF, 130–131

MULTIMEANING WORD CARDS, 143–146, 146f

MULTIPLE INTELLIGENCES THEORY, 133

MULTIPLE VOICES, POEMS FOR, 85, 87–92

MULTIPLYING MENACE (CALVERT), 170

MUMMY MATH (NEUSCHWANDER), 174

MURPHY, S.J., 46

MY EVEN DAY (FISHER & SNEED), 27, 28

MY HALF DAY (FISHER & SNEED), 171

N

NAGY, W.E., 105

NAHRANG, C.L., 50

NAPOLI, D.J., 174

NATARELLA, M.A., 70

NATIONAL CENTER FOR EDUCATION AND THE ECONOMY, 95

NATIONAL CENTER FOR EDUCATION STATISTICS, 11, 136

NATIONAL COUNCIL OF TEACHERS OF ENGLISH (NCTE), xi, 4, 7, 19, 33, 44, 69, 94, 100, 115, 129, 133, 137

NATIONAL COUNCIL OF TEACHERS OF MATHEMATICS (NCTM), ix, xi, 8, 44, 46, 48, 69, 133, 137

NEELD, E.C., 59, 61, 62

NEUSCHWANDER, C., 55, 174

NEWBERY MEDAL WINNERS, 26

NONVERBAL BEHAVIOR, RECOGNITION AND COMPREHENSION OF, 96–97

NORTON, D.E., 20, 33

NORTON, S.E., 20

NOTABLE CHILDREN'S TRADE BOOKS BOOKLIST, 26

NUTHALL, G., 5

NYSTRAND, M., 12–13

O

ODOM, S.L., 33

OMANSON, R.C., 78

ON THE SCALE, A WEIGHTY TALE (CLEARY), 47
ONE HUNDRED HUNGRY ANTS (PINCZES), 81
ONE MORE BUNNY (WALTON), 22
ONE ODD DAY (FISHER & SNEED), 28
O'NEILL, MARY, 71
ORAL LANGUAGE SKILLS: listening in
    classroom, 96–98; overview of, 3–4,
    94–96, 127–128. See also listening
    skills; talking skills
ORAL REPORTS, 154–158
O'REILLY, G., 173
OUT-OF-SCHOOL LITERACIES, ENHANCEMENT OF,
    135
OUTSTANDING SCIENCE TRADE BOOKS FOR
    STUDENTS K–12, 26
OVERBY, M., 131

P

PAPPAMIHIEL, N.E., 14–15
PAPPAS, T., 87–88
PARR, N.C., 162
PATTERNS IN PERU (NEUSCHWANDER), 174
PATTERSON, E.U., 19, 34, 35–37
PELLEGRINI, A.D., 100
PEN PAL LETTER WRITING, 60–61
PERFETTI, C.A., 78
PERKINS, D., 132
PERSUASIVE ADVERTISEMENTS, 148–149, 150f,
    151
PETERSON, B.T., 50
PHELPS, S.F., 5
PICTOGRAPHIC DRAWINGS, 152, 153
PICTURE DICTIONARIES, 143, 144f
PIECE=PART=PORTION (GIFFORD), 21
PINCZES, E.J., 81
PIRO, J.M., 162
PLAYS, 124–125, 158, 160–161
PLOT, EVALUATION OF, 31
POETRY: ABC poems, 75–76; benefits of
    development of language skills through,
    92; definition of, 67–68; formula
    poems, 70–80; "I Don't Understand"
    poems, 78–80; ."..Is" poems, 70–75;
    "I used to Think..., but Now I Know"
    poems, 76–78; mathematics and,
    69–70; for multiple voices, 85, 87–92;
    poetic puzzles, 80–84; power of, 67;

preposition poems, 84–87; rhyme and,
    67–68
POETRY BOOKS, 23
POLLARD-DURODOLA, S., 101
POLLY'S PEN PAL (MURPHY), 46
PRELUTSKY, JACK, 68
PREPOSITION POEMS, 84–87
PREREADING STRATEGY, QUICK-WRITES AS, 46
PRESENTATION OF CONTENT, 29
PRINCIPLES AND STANDARDS FOR SCHOOL
    MATHEMATICS (NCTM): commonalities
    of, 9–10; Communication standard, 9,
    44, 69–70, 167; Connections standard,
    9, 168; description of, 8; focus of, ix;
    Measurement standard, 46; Problem
    Solving standard, 9, 167; Reasoning and
    Proof standard, 9, 167; Representation
    standard, 9, 168; text of, 165–168;
    viewing and visual representation and,
    137; writing skills, 44
PRINT MEDIA, 34–38
PROBLEM SOLVING STANDARD (NCTM), 9, 167
PROCESS STANDARDS, 9
PROCESS WRITING, 57
PUBLIC SPEAKING, 94–95. See also formal
    mathematical talk
PUGALEE, D.K., 43
PURPOSE OF ACTIVITIES, ARTICULATION OF, 126
PUZZLES, POETIC, 80–84

Q

QUALITY OF MATERIALS, 21, 33–34
QUICK-WRITES, 45–49

R

RANKIN, J.L., 60
RAPHAEL, T.E., 105
RAPS, 124–125
READABILITY, EVALUATION OF, 32
READENCE, J.E., 146
READERS THEATRE, 161
READING: for authentic purposes, 19; lines of
    poetry chorally, 92; poems for multiple
    voices aloud, 90
THE READING TEACHER (JOURNAL), 26, 178
REASONING AND PROOF STANDARD (NCTM), 9,
    167

REED, M.T., 135
REESE, L., 15
REIF, L., 45
REISBERG, J.A., 175
REPRESENTATION STANDARD (NCTM), 9, 168
RESOURCES: books, 177–178; professional journals, 178–179
RHYME, AND POETRY, 67–68
RIDDLE-ICIOUS (LEWIS), 80
RIDDLES, SOLVING AND WRITING, 80–84
RILEY, J.G., 100
RINEHART, J., 5
RINEHART, S.D., 161
ROBB, L., 51
ROBINSON, E.K., 175
ROE, B.D., 158
ROSENBLATT, L.M., 97
ROSS, E.P., 158
ROUND IS A MOONCAKE (THONG), 21
ROUTMAN, R., 92

S

SAMPSON, M., 22
SARAMA, J., 132–133
SCAFFOLDING ENGLISH LEARNERS (ELs), 134–135
SCHIRO, M., 27
SCHNITZLEIN, D., 175
SCHWARTZ, D.M., 24, 46
SCHWARTZ, R.M., 105
THE SECRET LIFE OF MATH (MCCALLUM), 174
SEGUES, USING QUICK-WRITES AS, 47
SEMANTIC MAPPING, 105–106, 107*f*
SHARING WITH YOUNGER AUDIENCES, 59
SHERIDAN-THOMAS, H.K., 137
SHORT, K.G., 134
SIDELNICK, M.A., 136
SILVER, J.W., 43
SILVERS, P., 130
SILVERSTEIN, SHEL, 68
SIMPSON, J., 23
SIR CUMFERENCE AND THE FIRST ROUND TABLE (NEUSCHWANDER), 55
SIR CUMFERENCE AND THE ISLE OF IMMETER (NEUSCHWANDER), 174
SLATER, W.H., 78
SLOAT, T., 81

SMITH, J.A., 20
SMOLIN, L.I., 11, 129–130, 136
SNEED, D., 27, 28, 171
SNEED, J., 136
SOLVING: math mysteries, 102, 103*f*, 104–105; riddles, 80–81, 84; word problems, 138–139, 140*f*
SORT IT OUT! (MARICONDA), 28
SPAGHETTI AND MEATBALLS FOR ALL! A MATHEMATICAL STORY (BURNS), 169
"SPILL YOUR BRAINS" TECHNIQUE, 49
SPINA, S.U., 135
SPLITTING THE HERD (HARRIS), 172–173
STAHL, S., 100
STANDARDIZED TESTING, PREPARATION FOR, 13
STANDARDS FOR CONTENT AREAS: commonalities of, 9–10; technology incorporation and, 10–11
STANDARDS FOR THE ENGLISH LANGUAGE ARTS (IRA & NCTE): commonalities of, 9–10; diversity and, 11; literacy and, 4, 7–8; public speaking and, 94; Standards 4-6, 69; Standards 7 and 8, 115; Standard 10, 100; text of, 163–164; viewing and visual representation and, 137; writing skills, 44
STORY DRAMATIZATIONS, 160–161
STORY LINE OF TRADE BOOKS, 30, 32
STORYBOOKS, 23–24
STRICKLAND, D.S., 43
STRUGGLING READERS, ENCOURAGEMENT FOR, 136
STUDENT COLLABORATION, FACILITATION OF, 12–13
STYLES OF LEARNING, SUPPORT FOR, 16
SUMMARIES, USING QUICK-WRITES AS, 48
SVOBODA, M.L., 136

T

TABA, H., 111
TALKING SKILLS: in classroom, 98; formal mathematical talk, 116–125; guidelines for, 125–127; informal mathematical talk, 99–100; overview of, 3–4, 94–95. *See also* focused mathematical communication
TANG, G., 80–81, 175–176

Tanner, M.L., 18, 69
Taylor, D., 20
Teachers' Choice Award for the Classroom, 27
Teachers' Choices booklist, 26
Teaching and Learning Multiliteracies (Anstey & Bull), 130
Teaching Children Mathematics (journal), 178–179
technology, incorporation of, 10–11, 135–136
Terban, M., 144
Terhaar-Yonkers, M., 135
textbooks, mathematical, 18–19
Thong, R., 21
365 Penguins (Fromental), 172
Tompkins, G.E., 4, 67–68, 85, 87, 122, 131, 148
trade books: annotated bibliography of, 33–34, 169–176; class-created, 151–154, 153*f*; literary criteria for evaluation of, 31–33; mathematical criteria for evaluation of, 27–30; review of available, 25–26; talk about, 100–101
transmediation, 133–134
trivia hunt, 114–115
Turner, P., 24
20 Hungry Piggies (Harris), 172
Tyler, B.J., 161
Tysvaer, N., 131

U

University of Pittsburgh, Learning Research and Development Center, 95
U.S. Census Bureau, 15

V

Vacca, J.A.L., 102
Vacca, R.T., 102, 131, 134
Vardell, S.M., 92
varied activities, planning for, 127
Vaughn, S., 101
Venn diagrams, 106–108, 108*f*
verbal-visual word association strategy, 146–148, 147*f*
A Very Improbable Story (Einhorn), 171

viewing media: benefits of including in literacy, 132–136; definition of, 129; experiences for, 131; importance of, 129–130
Viorst, J., 24, 32
visibility of content, 29
visual communication of information: class-created books, 151–154, 153*f*; oral reports, 154–158; persuasive advertisements, 148–149, 150*f*, 151
visual literacy, 161–162
visual representation of information: benefits of including in literacy, 132–136; dramatic, 158–161; experiences for, 131; importance of, 4–5, 9, 129–130; reinforcement of word knowledge through, 137–148
vocabulary development, 78
Vygotsky, L.S., 69, 133

W

Walton, Rick, 22
Weaver, S., 158
Wells, M., 69
When I Was Little (Curtis), 76–77
White, T.G., 78
Williams, B.T., 131
Williams, P.C., 135
Williams, T.L., 131
Wilson, P., 70
Wishes, Lies, and Dreams (Koch), 76
The Wishing Club (Napoli), 174
Wolvin, A.D., 96
Wood, A., 159
Woodward, A., 18
Woodward, V.A., 161–162
word cards, multimeaning, 143–146, 146*f*
word knowledge, reinforcement of through visual representation: creative concepts, 139–141, 142*f*, 143*f*; multimeaning word cards, 143–146, 146*f*; overview of, 137–138; picture dictionaries, 141–143, 144*f*; solving word problems, 138–139, 140*f*; verbal-visual word association strategy, 146–148, 147*f*
word problems, solving, 138–139, 140*f*

WRITER'S BLOCK: cubing and, 61; topics and, 44

WRITING RIDDLES, 81–84

WRITING ROULETTE, 55–58

WRITING SKILLS: activities for, 44–45; admit/exit slips, 51–54; creative writing, 58–59; draft-quality writing, 54; informational writing, 59–65; integration of, 43–44; journal writing, 50–51; overview of, 65–66; quick-writes, 45–49; strengthening, 54–59

WRITING STYLE, EVALUATION OF, 31–32

Y

YOU CAN, TOUCAN (ADLER), 169

YOU READ TO ME, I'LL READ TO YOU (HOBERMAN), 89

YOUNG, T.A., 92

Z

ZACHARY ZORMER (REISBERG), 175

ZASLAVSKY, C., 24–25

ZERO IS THE LEAVES ON THE TREE (FRANCO), 172